Charlotte
Danielson

Enhancing Student Achievement

A Framework for
School Improvement

ASSOCIATION FOR SUPERVISION AND CURRICULUM DEVELOPMENT ALEXANDRIA,
VIRGINIA USA

Association for Supervision and Curriculum Development
1703 N. Beauregard St. • Alexandria, VA 22311-1714 USA
Telephone: 800-933-2723 or 703-578-9600 • Fax: 703-575-5400
Web site: http://www.ascd.org • E-mail: member@ascd.org

Cover art copyright © 2002 by ASCD.

ASCD publications present a variety of viewpoints. The views expressed or implied in this book should not be interpreted as official positions of the Association.

Printed in the United States of America.

November 2002 member book (pc). ASCD Premium, Comprehensive, and Regular members periodically receive ASCD books as part of their membership benefits. No. FY03-02.

ISBN: 0-87120-691-9   ASCD product no.: 102109   ASCD member price: $18.95   nonmember price: $22.95

Library of Congress Cataloging-in-Publication Data
Danielson, Charlotte.
    Enhancing student achievement : a framework for school improvement /
Charlotte Danielson.
        p. cm.
Includes bibliographical references (p.   ) and index.
    ISBN 0-87120-691-9 (alk. paper)
  1. School improvement programs. 2. Academic achievement. I. Title.
LB2822.8 .D37 2002
371.2—dc21
                                                2002013156

08 07 06 05 04 03 02   10 9 8 7 6 5 4 3 2 1

Enhancing Student Achievement
A Framework for School Improvement

Acknowledgments

I would like to thank the hundreds of educators with whom I have worked over the past 30 years for their dedication and perseverance in doing important work, frequently under challenging conditions. I have learned much from them, and continue to learn more.

In addition, I would like to express particular thanks to Darlene Axtel, Puala Bevan, Margaret Boot, Bernadette Cleland, Joyce McCleod, Albert Miller, Julie Rhodes, Lynn Sawyer, Connie Sims, and Ted Stilwill for reading an early draft of the manuscript and offering helpful suggestions, and to Bobbi Newman for her contributions to Chapter 3. The book is far stronger as a result of their contributions.

Introduction:
The Political Context of
School Improvement

We can, wherever and whenever we choose, success-
fully teach all children whose schooling is of interest to
us. We already know more than we need to do that.
Whether or not we do it must finally depend on how
we feel about the fact that we haven't so far.

—Ron Edmonds (1969)

It has been 20 years since the publication of *A Nation at Risk* sounded the alarm regarding the poor quality of America's schools. Those years have been filled with much hand-wringing ("where have we gone wrong?"); confirmation (international studies of achievement that show U.S. students scoring, at best, at about the middle of the pack for industrial nations); defensiveness ("schools are not as bad as all that"); and surveys of opinion (showing parents to be much more satisfied with their children's schools than are the college professors who inherit the students or the employers who hire them). Many policy solutions have been recommended, and some have even been implemented, including content standards and assessments for students—sometimes with serious consequences for nonachievement; increased testing for teachers entering the profession, with sanctions on the colleges that prepare

them; and school report cards and "league tables," published in newspapers, that show the relative success of different schools within a district or state. Every recent U.S. president has made education a top priority, and virtually all candidates for political office have policy recommendations to address the problem, as they interpret it. Education, in other words, is on the public radar screen as it has not been in a generation.

The renewed attention to education has coincided with a profound shift in the U.S. and global economies: a move away from (and transformation of) the extractive industries of agriculture, fishing, mining, and manufacturing and toward a more service- and information-based economy. The jobs and lifestyles for which we are or should be preparing students require increasing amounts of "knowledge work," for which our schools of the past were not well suited. Furthermore, given demographic and societal changes, schools of today are charged with much more than teaching "the basics" of "book learning" to students whose primary skills were acquired on the farm and in the factory, and reinforced by attitudes taught in the family and the church. Today's schools are asked to assume responsibility not only for academic skills, but also for the development of character, civic virtue, and artistic talent.

Moreover, educators and members of the public have finally begun to take seriously what has been known for decades: that average student achievement masks significant differences in learning among different groups of students. These differences are related to both class and ethnicity; indeed, it is hard to disentangle them from one another. But the uncomfortable truth is this: poor or minority students, who are overwhelmingly enrolled in schools with the fewest resources and the least qualified teachers, achieve at levels far below those of white, middle-class students, however those achievement levels are measured. This fact is not new. What *is* new is the general recognition that we are not serving our students well, and that we have an ethical obligation to assist all students in realizing their full potential. The health of the U.S. economy and the profitability of U.S. companies depend in large measure on the skill level of the workforce; there are, therefore, both ethical and economic imperatives for all students to be schooled at a level once reserved for the privileged few. This recognition has fueled the current insistence on standards-based reform, with its implicit corollary that the content and quality of student learning is a matter for public discourse and policy. The policies being proposed and implemented reflect public frustration that after 20 years of effort, there is so little widespread or lasting improvement to show for it. With a few important exceptions, student achievement has not significantly improved since 1983, and the achievement gap between students in different neighborhoods and of different backgrounds persists. This lack of progress is the result, in part, of educators' ten-

dency to flirt with new initiatives without fundamentally changing how they manage the core functions of teaching and learning.

The models and rubrics that I offer in this book are intended to help educators to seriously examine these core functions. This, however, is not enough: educators must also bear in mind that there is a political subtext to the effort. After all, public schools take public money, which makes them accountable to elected officials at the state and local level. Decisions made regarding schools—the regulations on curriculum and testing, teacher licensing and certification, and the allocation of resources—are all influenced by political considerations. This effectively means that in addition to *knowing* the right way to improve schools, educators and the public must truly *want* to do so. Knowledge, in other words, must be accompanied by political will.

To a large extent, political will is reflected in dollars and cents. Societies tend to allocate public funds to activities that they value, such as warplanes, highways and bridges, farm supports, and the arts. In schools, this funding is usually directed toward new programs or smaller classes. Of course, not everything worth doing costs money—such as when elementary school teachers decide to form instructional teams, for example, or when high school teachers take on larger classes so that one of them can be free each period to assist struggling students. People must *want* to improve their schools whether or not it costs money to do so, and must be convinced that the effort will pay off. In addition, they must be certain that their actions are ethically sound—that what they are doing is *right*.

Unfortunately, the track record of American schools and communities on this last point is not particularly encouraging.

Twenty-three percent of all high school teachers never even minored in their main teaching field. For math teachers, the number rises to over 30 percent, and both figures are higher in schools that serve economically disadvantaged students. In schools with mostly nonwhite students, 54 percent of math and science teachers are certified in their field, and only 42 percent hold a bachelor's degree in the field. The comparable numbers for teachers in predominantly white schools are, respectively, 86 percent and 69 percent. In addition, many schools assign teachers to teach a section or two in fields for which they have no background at all. The scarcity of well-qualified teachers might have something to do with teacher salaries, which are far lower than those of other professions that require a significant level of preparation, such as accountants, registered nurses, and social workers (National Commission on Teaching and America's Future, 1996).

The degree of public investment in schools varies tremendously across the country; expenditures in the Northeast, for example, far exceed those of the Deep South. To some extent, these disparities reflect the different costs of living in each region, although they exist within states, too: in 1997, for instance, the schools with the highest per-pupil expenditure in New York State spent over $8,000 per student, while those with the lowest spent only $5,300—a difference of $2,700 per pupil, or a million dollars for a school with 400 students (Education Trust Data Bulletin, 2001).

Myths About U.S. Society

The United States is a society organized around many powerful ideas and myths. It is the land of opportunity and freedom, with a political philosophy embodied in the Constitution and the Bill of Rights. Immigrants are drawn to the United States by the political and religious freedom it affords, as well as to earn decent wages; they also come because they perceive the United States to be a classless society, where advancement is determined not by the social standing of one's family, by one's accent, or by the traditional occupations of one's forebears. The U.S. claim, as a society, is that success is based on merit, without regard to an individual's inherited status.

Compared to many other societies, the United States is indeed free of class distinctions. U.S. history is filled with stories of people from humble origins rising to positions of enormous power, influence, and responsibility, both in the public and private spheres.

In spite of the mythology, however, U.S. society is not nearly as open and free as some would suggest, or as many immigrants believe. Even in the United States, privilege begets privilege; some people have a significant advantage as they seek their place in the economic and social order. Some of these advantages are described below.

A System of Informal Expectations

Students with well-educated families and friends often hear that they are expected to "make something of themselves." These suggestions can take many forms: A 7th grader's cousin may ask whether he is taking algebra yet, for instance, or a high school junior's best friend might ask whether she has applied to college yet. These questions are grounded in knowledge as well as expectations: the 7th grader's cousin knows that an early start in algebra can open doors later on, and the junior's best friend knows that college plans should be made well in advance.

Students with less educated families and friends may never be asked the above questions. Poorly educated parents may be unfamiliar with the ways of the educational system, and therefore in no position to ensure access to a higher education for their children. They may recognize that education is a key to future success, and their own experiences in school may have been positive, but they may not be aware of the importance of algebra, for example, or of studying a second language. The children of such parents don't have the benefit of family advocates looking out for their educational interests.

Because of this disparity between students from well-educated families and those with less knowledgeable parents, high school teachers have a particular responsibility to help all students to determine their future plans. Most high schools have counselors, of course, whose explicit responsibility it is to provide guidance regarding such decisions. These individuals can play a critical role in students' lives, helping them to see new possibilities and overcome discouragement in their daily class work. However, counselors typically have a large number of students assigned to them, thereby limiting one-on-one interaction. Furthermore, many counselors' roles consist only of course registration and conflict resolution. Still counselors can have a tremendous effect; college is simply not on the radar screen for some students, and an encouraging word from a respected counselor can literally alter the course of their lives.

Of course, school counselors can't do everything—they don't see the students every day, and they are not aware of the quality of the students' daily work. Teachers, however, do and are, and therefore are in an excellent position to encourage student ambitions. When teachers take an interest in students' lives outside of the classroom—by attending athletic events or school plays, for instance, or by reading the school newspaper— they let students know that they are making important contributions to the life of the school. Such support might be more than the students receive from any other source.

Informal Access to Opportunity

Members of the economic and political elite tend to look after their own, and are inclined to offer opportunities to others like themselves. When privileged young adults make their career choices, they can contact relatives or friends of the family to learn about different occupations and the education required to pursue them; when applying for jobs, they may be granted interviews because of family connections. Some of the enhanced opportunities of the privileged are well established and even institutionalized: some colleges, for instance, give special consideration to descendants of alumni—or "legacies," in academic parlance— during the application process.

The informal access to opportunity that some individuals enjoy is frequently invisible, even to those who benefit from it. Thus students from poor backgrounds, whose families are not in a position to offer them substantive assistance as they embark on their life's journey, may sense that the system is not quite fair without being able to point out why. Similarly, more privileged students might not necessarily recognize that their peers don't all enjoy the same advantages; they may well assume that they have achieved their successes on their own merits. As a pundit once said about a well-heeled politician, such a student "was born on third base and thought he hit a triple."

Informal access to opportunity begins at an early age. Elementary school PTAs and PTOs are composed largely of parents (principally mothers) who are ambitious for their children and want to ensure that they benefit from skilled teachers, enrichment classes, and "gifted" status. Although such parents often make material contributions to their children's schools, they are also a force to be reckoned with, because they are accustomed to getting their way on behalf of their children.

At the middle and high school level, the influence of highly involved parents takes a slightly different form. They do their best to ensure that their children are enrolled in algebra at the first opportunity, and they make certain that their children take advanced courses and participate in activities that will look good on their college applications.

The Language of Power

George Bernard Shaw's *Pygmalion* was based on the idea that class—and therefore opportunities in life—depends on one's manner of speech. In Shaw's play, a lower-class English girl "passes" as an Austrian countess after being taught how to speak "properly" by an upper-class gentleman. Of course, *Pygmalion* was set in Britain, where language has traditionally been a more important indicator of class and status than in the United States. But even in the United States there exists "Standard English," which is spoken as a matter of course in middle- and upper-class homes. Of course, other types of English are spoken in the United States as well, including "black English"

and rural dialects. I should note that these are true languages, with vocabularies and syntax that differ somewhat from those of Standard English.

The variety of types of English has serious social and instructional implications for children, many of whom are encouraged by their teachers to abandon their dialects for Standard English when they enter school. These teachers are for the most part well intentioned; they know that it is important for their students to speak the language of the middle class. But unless they are careful, they can convey to their students the sense that their backgrounds or cultures, as embodied in their language, are inferior to those of other students. Some students find themselves confronted with making a (false) choice between their own cultures and the culture of school.

Children who enter school speaking a dialect other than Standard English find that they are, in effect, in an "immersion classroom," learning what for them is a different language. Learning to read and write is a greater challenge for such students than it is for those who speak Standard English at home. The fact that many of these students can hold their ground in the early years of school is a testament to their intelligence and drive. In the later years, when correct usage and grammar become important topics in the language arts classroom, grammatical constructions will sound "right" to students who have grown up in households where Standard English is spoken, but will have to be memorized by others as they would a second language.

The type of English students speak will affect their chances in the job market as well as at school. Most employers will insist that their employees speak "correctly" using Standard

English. Hence, mastery of Standard English is an essential life skill for students, and one that carries enormous implications for their future success.

The Sense of Privilege and Entitlement

Students from privileged backgrounds often assume that they will inherit access to opportunity virtually as a birthright. They are accustomed to doors opening for them, and are frequently afforded second and third chances when they make mistakes. Less privileged students, on the other hand, learn to be wary, due either to personal experiences or community lore. Students who expect things to break their way frequently find that they do, partly because the expectations themselves grant them self-confidence; informal access to opportunity and mastery of the language of power tend to reinforce these positive expectations.

The Cycle of Poverty and Ignorance

Poverty and ignorance have become increasingly linked over the past decades. During the economic boom immediately following World War II, an individual with an 8th grade education could support a family, buy a house and car, and pay college tuition with the wages from a factory job.

Today, the situation is quite different: automobile mechanics, medical technicians, and office assistants make use of sophisticated electronic equipment; modern farmers engage in extensive analyses of factors of production; and assembly-line workers solve complex problems with other members of their production teams. Low-skilled jobs exist, to be sure, but they pay wages far lower than necessary for a middle-class lifestyle: many

U.S. citizens living below the poverty level are employed but unable to earn enough money to support themselves, much less a family. Those trying to support a family are obliged to work two or even three jobs, juggling multiple demands on their time, and with virtually no margin for misfortune. Furthermore, low-wage jobs for the uneducated tend to be dead ends, with little or no possibility of advancement.

The *cycle* of poverty and ignorance is unrelenting. Those without an education cannot find well-paying jobs and are thus trapped in poverty; their children, in turn, grow up poor and without the resources or contacts to improve their prospects, and thus are ineligible to compete for the high-skill, high-wage jobs of the information age. (For underprivileged black students, slim prospects are made even slimmer by institutional racism.) Thus the cycle continues, broken only occasionally by people with good fortune or extraordinary perseverance.

Breaking the Cycle

Schools have a particular responsibility to break the cycle of poverty and ignorance, because it is through education that young people can escape from their apparent destinies. Schools cannot of course replicate the more subtle forms of privilege from which some students benefit—namely, the access to information and people of influence. But they must ensure that all students acquire a solid basic education and are able to use their minds. Schools can also ensure that the doors to further education are truly open to all students—that they not only have the knowledge and skill to be eligible for higher education, but that they are fully aware of their options and how to gain access to them.

Allocating Resources

It is unconscionable that resources are not evenly allocated to schools serving different populations, even within the same community. It is indefensible for schools in more affluent neighborhoods to be equipped with more modern equipment and books, larger libraries, and more qualified teachers than those in poor neighborhoods. A community that would allow such practices to persist cannot be truly committed to equal educational opportunities for all students. A case could easily be made that resources to schools serving different populations be unequal, but only if the majority of resources went to schools serving less privileged students.

Ensuring the Success of All Students

This book is dedicated to helping educators to organize their efforts so that all students, not only those from affluent backgrounds, acquire the knowledge and skills necessary for success. But ensuring successful learning for all demands more than technical skill; it also requires persistence and unwavering commitment and may require everyone involved to go against the grain of expectations. Schools can help break the cycle of lowered expectations by making good on their commitment to ensure that every student leaves school with the knowledge and skill to continue learning and achieving at high levels.

Teaching the Language of Power

In order to break out of the cycle of poverty and ignorance, students must become fluent in Standard English, but not at the expense of stu-

dents' confidence or pride in their own backgrounds and cultures. Some schools manage to do this by clearly differentiating between "school language" and "home language": teachers convey their belief that "home language" is rich and legitimate, but that everyone must speak "school language" in school. Students who have learned "school language" as a second language are effectively bilingual and can make their way in several distinct environments; and by becoming fluent in "school language," they become enormously confident in their skills as learners. This confidence can serve them well as they tackle challenging material; neither they nor their teachers will be inclined to give up when difficulties arise. Confidence in one's skill as a learner is a lifelong gift that students gain from school, and it can start in the acquisition of a new language.

Replicating Informal Expectations

Schools cannot replicate the natural advantage that privileged students derive from family connections, but they *can* help to even the playing field. For example, teachers in a middle school can teach their students that school does not end with a high school diploma, and that one of the purposes of high school is to explore different content areas to determine a field of concentration for college; similarly, high schools can ensure that all students are aware of scholarship opportunities, deadlines and testing requirements for college admissions, and the procedures for securing faculty recommendations. Although many high schools do make such information available, they do not make an effort to ensure that all students take advantage of it. It is not enough to have brochures available in an office, when some students won't know to go there. The information must go *to* the students, through an aggressive campaign of awareness and career planning. *All* students, not just those whose parents can offer to help them without the school's assistance, must be encouraged to see their current education as only the beginning of their search for higher levels of skill and knowledge.

Sustaining the Political Commitment to Breaking the Cycle

Educators must develop and sustain the political commitment to letting all students have a fair shot at a better life than that of their parents. Of course, it is more of a challenge to ensure success for all students and to help them develop confidence when working with few resources. Still, most of the factors contributing to student learning are a matter of attitude rather than money—of allocating existing resources for maximum effect, insisting on high-quality teaching and learning, and, above all, of instilling the culture of success in every aspect of a school's operations.

Summary

The early 21st century is an exciting and challenging era for education. Many stars are in alignment: heightened awareness, legislative mandates, and validated approaches. Beyond the economic rationale, educators have an ethical imperative to help all students realize their highest potential and break the cycle of poverty and ignorance. After all, if educators don't do this, who will? Educators cannot sit back and wait for others to act. They must do what only *they* can do—namely, ensure that every child who enters school leaves with a solid education and the skills and confidence to do something with it.

➤ ➤ ➤

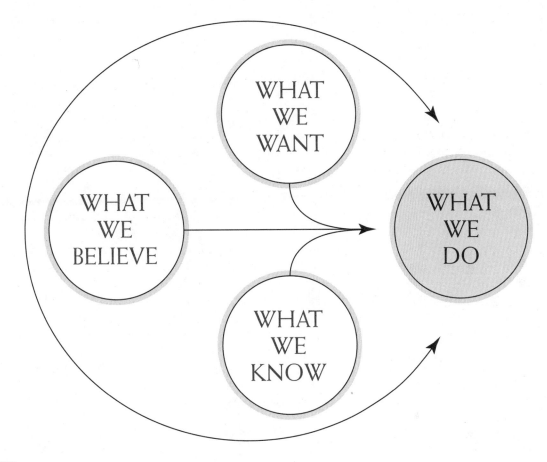

Part 1:

The Four Circles Model

Truly comprehensive school improvement measures must take into account the goals and values of practitioners as well as the most up-to-date research in the field. In other words, decisions regarding what we do—i.e., implementation of the framework presented in Part 2—must be predicated on consensus about what we want, what we believe, and what we know. Chapters 1–3 provide educators with a systemic approach to considering each of these issues separately; Chapter 4 suggests ways to coordinate objectives, beliefs, and the research literature in the service of student learning.

1

What We Want

"We are so lucky—our children go to a very good school."

"I want to transfer to West High; it's a much better school than Overlake."

Comments like these are heard frequently, in backyard conversations as well as in the faculty lounge. Those who make them have ideas about what constitutes a "good" school, although they do not typically state these opinions explicitly. It is important, however, to do so; only if we know what specifically we *mean* by "good" can we hope to achieve it.

So what *is* a "good" school? It depends on whom you ask, of course, and whether you mean good for students or good for educators. Consider, for example, how responses would differ depending on whether the following questions were put to teachers or to parents:

Question posed to parents: *If you were to walk into a school, what might you see or hear there that would cause you to say to yourself: "I would like my own child to attend this school"?*

Possible answers:

➤ It's a safe place: there are no frayed electrical wires, for instance, and children aren't afraid to go outside.
➤ It's a happy place: students are treated well.
➤ Children aren't bullied by other students.
➤ The teaching is good: the children learn.

3

➤ Test scores show good results.

➤ Teachers care about students.

Question posed to teachers: *If you were to walk into a school, what might you see or hear there that would cause you to say to yourself: "I would like to work here"?*

Possible answers:

➤ Teachers have their own classrooms.

➤ Administrators listen to teachers' views.

➤ Students come to class prepared and ready to learn; teachers don't have to waste a lot of time on behavioral issues.

➤ Teachers don't have to spend a lot of time in meetings.

➤ Teachers are given a chance to learn from their colleagues.

These types of answers, while sincere, can't serve as the sole basis for school improvement: they may need to be collected and analyzed, then used as the foundation of an action plan. Of course, many schools have not taken the time or trouble to do this. They have instead continued along, defining their aims imprecisely, engaging in "business as usual" without recognizing that some of their practices actually work in opposition to their goals. In truth, "business as usual" has been good enough for some schools: those in affluent communities, where parents have high expectations for their children and are able to offer them educational opportunities outside of school, post state test scores or acceptance notices to selective colleges that make the schools look good, and be considered superior by the public and the professional community.

Still, even good schools can improve, and many schools are not succeeding by any standards. The first step toward improving any school is to be absolutely clear about "what it wants." Goals serve as a school's set of organizing principles; they are a way for the school to define its direction. Only if educators can be clear about what they intend to accomplish can they actually hope to do so. While it is tempting, in this era of renewed accountability and high-stakes assessment, to set "improved student test scores" as a goal, this is not sufficient because test scores reflect a school's other characteristics, such as high-level learning and a positive learning environment. Therefore, decisions about "what we want"—while almost certainly bound to encompass improved student performance on high-stakes tests—should be considered within the broader context of overall school improvement.

Goals to Include in "What We Want"

The purpose of schools is to teach students; whatever else they do, they must promote high-level student learning. The public, along with the school boards and legislators it elects, will not tolerate schools that do not prepare students to achieve at high levels. All schools, therefore, must clearly specify their goals for student learning in ways that make sense to their stakeholders.

Most schools have other goals in addition to student learning, relating perhaps to the school environment for teachers and students, or to the role of the school in the larger community. Most of these goals are not in opposition to one another— they may even be complementary—but they are distinct and should be articulated separately.

Schools and school communities must determine their goals for themselves. This is not work that people can do for one another. Consequently, the discussion that follows is merely a draft of ideas that school staff might consider when developing goals; it is intended to provide grist for the mill of conversation. Most school communities will probably find that they will want to include some version of the following among their goals:

➤ High-level learning for all students

➤ A safe, attractive, and positive environment

➤ A culture of hard work and opportunity

➤ A school that functions as a learning environment for the faculty and a center of learning within the larger community

School communities might consider other broad areas for improvement, of course. These are offered simply to get the conversation going.

We Want: High-Level Learning for All Students

At the very least, schools must provide for the learning of students—*all* students. Three questions immediately emerge from this statement:

➤ Why is it important to help *all* students learn, and what do we even mean by "all students"?

➤ What is "high-level learning"? What does it include? Does it reflect an elitist view of education? How does it relate to state or district curriculum standards, or to high-stakes tests that students may be required to take?

➤ What would count as evidence of success for each aspect of the statement?

Many states have provided at least a partial answer to the last two questions by effectively legislating high-level learning to mean student performances that meet the standards set by state assessments. The states back up their expectations of students through a combination of carrots, such as bonuses for schools that perform well, and sticks, such as reduced funding (or even state takeovers) for schools that don't measure up.

A school district's operational definition of "high-level learning" is, typically, its curriculum. Despite the state's involvement, there are many important curriculum decisions to be made at the local level. Not everything of value is included on state tests, so educators must decide for themselves whether to offer certain subjects—a particular book, for example, or a music course—to their students. In addition, schools must translate state content standards, and the demands of the tests designed to measure them, into concrete curriculum expectations.

Let's now examine each of these matters in turn, identifying some of the issues educators might want to consider when discussing high-level learning.

All students. More than 200 years ago, Thomas Jefferson pointed out the critical importance of an educated citizenry to the survival of a democracy. It is essential to the health of the republic that citizens be literate, so that they can participate actively in the political process and analyze candidate positions in order to make informed judgments and vote intelligently. When candidates can appeal to fear and ignorance, democracy is threatened.

More recently, analysts have identified the cognitive skills required by workers in a global economy organized around information technology. As they point out, millions of workers in other parts of the world are willing to perform low-skilled work for minimal wages. If we are to have a high-wage society, citizens must be able to perform high-skilled work.

There are also ethical and moral reasons for teaching all students well. For better or worse, success in school is a ticket to opportunity in the wider world. Escaping from poverty virtually always necessitates at least a high-school diploma, and usually much more. In addition, one's sense of self—the degree of confidence with which one approaches new challenges—is reflective of past success. For most people, therefore, school success—or the lack thereof—is an essential component of their identity.

Of course, educators know that school success is not expected of some students, while for others it appears to be an entitlement. Students themselves have varying expectations regarding school, reflecting the attitudes of their homes and communities, or perhaps previous school experiences; the initially high hopes of some students might have been undermined over time by low expectations and an unchallenging curriculum. Ensuring the success of all students in school, then, requires vigilance on the part of teachers and administrators, and may require a significant shift in attitude on the part of some educators.

High-level learning. Of course! It almost goes without saying that all students need high-level learning. Given the remarkable societal changes of the past half-century, it is preposterous to try to predict with any accuracy the specific knowledge and skills that today's students will need in the future—for example, who could have foreseen, a generation ago, the transformation of the position of secretary? Who would have guessed that auto mechanics, assembly-line workers, and farmers would one day need sophisticated computer-technology skills? What we *can* be sure of is that some basic knowledge and skills will always be necessary, along with the high-level cognitive skills of critical thinking, communication, problem-solving, collaboration, and—above all—the skill of learning new skills.

These high-level cognitive skills are required for good citizenship as well. This vision is not elitist. As New York Justice Leland DeGrasse explained in deciding a 2001 court case:

> A capable and productive citizen doesn't simply turn up for jury service. Rather, she is capable of serving impartially on trials that may require learning unfamiliar facts and concepts and new ways to communicate and reach decisions with her fellow jurors. To be sure . . . life experience and practical intelligence can be more important than formal education. Nonetheless, jurors may be called on to decide complex matters that require the verbal, reasoning, math, science, and socialization skills that should be imparted in public schools. Jurors today must determine questions of fact concerning DNA evidence, statistical analyses, and convoluted financial fraud, to name only three topics (Archibold, 2001).

Justice DeGrasse's vision of a 21st-century jury reinforces the "all students" imperative: any citizen may be called to jury duty and, once there, must be able to exercise high-level skills.

Most people would add other types of learning to high-level cognitive skills, too, such as interpersonal skills (e.g., respect, tolerance, and compassion), dispositions (perseverance, patience, and curiosity), and sound judgment regarding aesthetics, ethics, and a sense of civic responsibility. Students must be taught to enjoy what they have learned to do: it is not sufficient that students learn to read; they must also want to do it. Similarly, it is not enough for citizens to be capable of analyzing candidate positions on issues; they must also be inclined to vote in an election.

Evidence of success. No discussion of school goals can proceed very far without serious consideration of assessment. That is, what would count as evidence of progress toward or achievement of goals? It makes no sense to have goals in place without being able to measure to what extent they have been achieved; only when such gauges are established can further action be planned. Any determination of school goals, therefore, must be accompanied by the corresponding question: How will we know if we are achieving them?

What would count as evidence of high-level learning? When should it be made available, and to whom? How should it be used? Standardized assessments, by which I mean multiple-choice, machine-scorable tests, can provide schools with information about students' acquisition of basic knowledge and cognitive skills. Many states and districts require standardized assessments of their students in order to effectively evaluate school pro-

grams. Such information can be extremely valuable, and when the results are disaggregated by various factors—such as gender, ethnicity, and socioeconomic status—they can indicate the extent to which the school is meeting its obligation to educate all students to at least a basic level.

Standardized assessments can be administered inexpensively to large numbers of students, and they allow for a school to be evaluated against a much wider population. Yet despite their strengths, they can measure only a relatively small percentage of desired learning, and they are notoriously ill-suited to measuring higher-order skills, such as writing fluently and expressively, formulating and testing hypotheses, recognizing patterns, evaluating information, designing experiments, and solving complex problems. If a school allows its success to be defined by state-mandated standardized assessments, and directs the instructional program solely toward improving scores on those assessments, it will necessarily limit the range of student experience in school. Consequently, standardized measures of achievement should be only one among many ways for educators to gauge their instructional success.

What else, then, constitutes evidence of high-level learning by students? It depends, of course, on how that learning is defined—for example, whether it includes skills in reasoning, writing fluency, or problem solving. Some higher-order skills, such as writing, can be reliably measured if the assessment methods are thoughtfully designed and consistently applied. For example, a group of teachers might decide on a level of persuasive writing and set it as a standard for students in their grade; by crafting assignments and rubrics according to this standard, the teachers would then be able to reliably and consistently assess their students' writing levels. The creation and use of these kinds of assessments to chart student progress can help educators to further focus school-improvement efforts.

Of course, some important outcomes of schooling do not lend themselves to formal assessment at all, much less to standardized, multiple-choice, machine-scorable tests. Different types of indicators would be necessary to assess, for example, such dispositions as perseverance, respect for the views of others, and aesthetic discernment. In such cases, less formal assessments may prove useful: teachers know perseverance (or a lack thereof) when they see it, and they can use informal records to engage students, parents, and colleagues in important dialogue.

We Want: A Safe, Attractive, and Positive Environment

Most educators and members of the public would agree that they want their schools to be safe, positive, and respectful places.

Physical safety and building appearance. Students must be protected from violence and falling ceilings, and some schools must be equipped with metal detectors. In addition to being physically safe, however, schools should also be aesthetically appealing: a school's appearance sends a powerful message to students and families about the value educators place on their students' well-being.

Positive interpersonal environment. It is not only the physical environment, of course, that must be conducive to learning; the interpersonal environment must contribute as well. Students must be

treated with respect and dignity, and rules and procedures must be developed to honor their autonomy and integrity. Most educators recognize the subtle influence of institutional regulations on the school culture; with this in mind, they should consider the following questions:

➤ How do teachers and other staff treat the students?

➤ When students go to the office, are they kept waiting while the office staff gossips?

➤ Are student requests treated as unwelcome interruptions?

➤ Are all students regarded as either real or potential troublemakers?

➤ Are students permitted to assume genuine responsibility for their achievements?

➤ Are the rules for attendance and homework sufficiently flexible to accommodate individual circumstances?

➤ Are students permitted to establish and maintain a culture that systematically discriminates against their peers?

➤ Are bullying and its effects on its victims tolerated?

We Want: A Student Culture of Hard Work and Opportunity

Schools are not places for amusement and relaxation, but rather for important learning, which requires rigor, perseverance, and self-discipline—in other words, hard work. But learning can also be gratifying, intellectually stimulating, and *fun*. In addition to bequeathing to students the gift of mastery over difficult content, educators must grant them *the sense that they can master* difficult content; this confidence gives students an essential feeling of power over their world.

A positive interpersonal environment can exist only within a highly respectful school culture that treats all students with dignity and delegates to them responsibilities appropriate to their level of maturity. The school culture should also be businesslike, with teachers and students sharing the sense that their work is important and relevant, both at present and in the longer term. Finally, the school must foster the idea that hard work will be rewarded: educators need to show students that, if they make a serious commitment to school, they can be successful.

We Want: A Learning Center for the Faculty and Larger Community

Schools should be places of learning for educators and for adults in the larger community as well as for students.

A professional learning community. In order to provide students with the best possible learning opportunities, teachers must continuously work to advance their knowledge and skills. Most educators want to work in a place that meets their professional needs; like their students, they seek opportunities for learning that will be relevant in both the short and long term. As with the culture for student learning, this emphasis on professional development is embedded in the norms and values of the school—in the priorities for recognition and funding, for example. Professional development must consist of more than one-shot workshops, or checking off boxes on a license renewal application; it must enable teachers to engage in meaningful work with their colleagues to strengthen their knowledge and skills for the complex challenges of teaching.

A culture of professional inquiry can be reflected both in teacher activities and in their attitudes toward one another and their work. For example, in some schools, teachers essentially work alone and their interactions with colleagues consist primarily of attending to "business," such as scheduling parent conferences, coordinating the implementation of a new discipline policy, or debating the use of a certain textbook. The essential aspects of their work—teaching and interacting with students—are conducted in isolation. In these schools, any suggestion that teachers might want to observe one another at work can be seen as threatening, or as an indication of deficiency. In a school committed to professional learning, teachers might identify aspects of their practice that could be improved—leading class discussions, for instance—and then ask to observe colleagues in action, not to provide them with feedback (as in a supervisory or coaching relationship), but *to learn from them.* In these schools, teachers are recognized as the professional resources they are, and structures are in place so that all teachers can access these resources. These structures might include study groups, time set aside to observe one another at work and discuss the design and implementation of challenging lessons, and regular opportunities for teachers to describe their work more generally to the entire faculty. A culture of professional inquiry should support teacher interaction and dialogue. Teachers who engage in serious discussions about their practice should be regarded as committed to their profession, not as deficient or weak. The school expectation should be that *everyone* is engaged in learning.

To promote a culture of professional inquiry, structures and expectations must be established, and time allocated to them. Attitudes should welcome professional interaction and conversation, and all teachers should be engaged in professional activities with their colleagues. These things can be monitored and improved.

A learning center for the larger community. Public schools are supported by public money, and they exist to serve the public. Historically, their mission has been to educate the children of a community. However, in these days of the "new economy," everybody is a lifelong learner: adults frequently must assume new job responsibilities or change careers, which requires learning new skills, whether at universities and community colleges or through less formal means. In addition, many adults regard learning as recreational—an opportunity to learn how to paint or draw, speak another language, or play a musical instrument.

Many schools serve as beacons for adult learning in their communities, and offer a wide variety of courses to local residents, be they academic, technical, or hobby-related. The classrooms and computer labs are already in place, so why not use them for a "second shift" after 4:00 p.m.? The school library may even contain resources not available at the community public library. Of course, the use of school facilities by community groups presents record-keeping and operational challenges. Who will provide custodial services and ensure that the building is locked? Will the different users share supplies, such as paper for the computer printers? If so, how will the costs be allocated? If not, where will each group store its supplies, and how will they have access to them? The list of possible obstacles is long, and for some would constitute sufficient reason to not even try using school facilities after-hours. In this, as in much else connected with school improvement, a problem-solving attitude is critical: "This is what we want to do," educators must say to themselves. "Now let's figure out how to do it."

Summary

A school's articulation of what it wants—of its goals for itself and for its students—provides a blueprint for everything else it works to achieve. Without clarity on these matters, no school can hope to move forward; educators will certainly be busy, but they won't be making any progress. A set of clear goals—sometimes referred to as a mission—allows a school's staff to focus its energies in support of what the school wants, and provides a standard by which to analyze whether established policies and practices are helping the school achieve its goals. Goals, in other words, provide schools with a framework for action.

➤ ➤ ➤

2 | What We Believe

An essential "filter" for a school's operations is its belief structure—the guiding principles that influence all aspects of its program. Some of these beliefs are grounded in research; others are not. Whatever the case, beliefs guide the thinking not only of school staff, but of students and parents as well; when stated explicitly, beliefs can fuel a school's vision, enabling all in the school to come together around a common purpose.

The beliefs held by staff cast a very long shadow over school practices. In fact, in order to create a school in which all students fulfill their learning potential, the school staff must accept a certain set of beliefs and perspectives regarding the school, its culture, and its students, and must implement policies and practices based on those beliefs. If educators approach challenges in a fatalistic, rather than problem-solving, manner—if they take the view, for example, that "these kids just aren't good in math"—then their students will almost certainly fail.

So what types of beliefs might find their way into a school's philosophy and have the potential to drive practice? What staff attitudes, if universally adopted, might set the stage for a school culture of learning and success? First and foremost, the entire staff of a school must believe that its mission is to ensure success of all students. Failure is not an option, neither for students nor staff. The job of a school is to ensure that all students learn well and master the established curriculum standards. There are a number of different aspects to this "success orientation," as will be seen. But the overall concept is simple: the job of everyone in the school—students, teachers, administrators, classi-fied staff—is to make certain that everyone achieves at high levels.

Of the various beliefs supporting a good school, a focus on success is by far the most important; no other belief comes close to matching it as an organizing principle for action. The differ-ent components of this success orientation are described below. (Although I discuss them sepa-rately here, these components are not independent of one another in practice, but rather intertwined in multiple ways.)

We Believe: That Human Beings Are Learning Organisms

Human beings are learning organisms—this is a fact. As such, it is part of "what we know." Preschool children never fail at learning, as is demonstrated by their acquisition of language. Of course, some children learn to talk sooner than oth-ers, but eventually all of them do, with vocabularies of between 3,000 and 10,000 words by the time they enter school. And talking is an extraordinarily complex learning task: of the skills we acquire over our lifetimes, learning to talk is probably the most complicated and demanding, extending beyond vocabulary to include syntax and rules of grammar. In fact, the errors young children make—e.g., "Are all the mans coming to the picnic?"—reflect their having already absorbed important rules of usage. Nothing else we ever learn even approaches learn-ing to speak in difficulty, yet children of two, three, and four years of age learn to do so all the time.

Children also learn, at an early age, the many spoken and unspoken rules that prescribe behav-ior in their culture (for example, they learn to be polite—at least in public—before their elders). In addition, young children learn hundreds of facts and relationships among facts. They learn about the patterns of life in their community: who comes and goes, how they behave, why they should wear shoes in some situations but not in others, how to tell the mailman from a policeman, and so on. In other words, preschool children are effective and efficient learners; this is what everyone expects them to be, and this is what they are.

Though we *know* that human beings are learn-ing organisms, we also must *believe* it. If the adults in a school truly *believe* that all children are natural learners, then they are likely to establish practices different from those they would employ in the absence of this belief. If educators truly believe that all children are natural learners, then when-ever a student encounters difficulty—as virtually all students will—teachers are likelier to try ascer-taining the cause of the difficulty to see that it is overcome. Educators without such a belief, on the other hand, are much more likely to give up and find something, or more likely someone, to blame. Hence the phenomenon of ascribing students' learning failure to such factors as their poverty or their parents' lack of education. These factors might explain the degree to which a child *has* learned outside of school, but say nothing about what she still *can* learn.

The belief in the natural capacity of all chil-dren to learn well must of course be accompanied by the next belief:

We Believe: That Success in All Endeavors Is the Result of Hard Work, Luck, and Natural Endowment

Numerous research studies have found that American students attribute their successes and failures in school to different factors than do their European and Asian peers (Stevenson, 1990). American students report that, if they succeed at a task, it is because they are "good" at the subject; when they do poorly, it is because they are not "good" at it, or because the teacher doesn't like them, or perhaps because they were simply unlucky. Students in other countries, by contrast, attribute their successes to hard work, and a lack of success to insufficient effort on their part.

A sense of efficacy helps students feel empowered; those who believe that the factors influencing their successes and failures are beyond their control, on the other hand, can become paralyzed and fatalistic. If students truly believe that unalterable natural endowment is all that matters, they will tend to give up easily. If, however, they are taught that effort *does* make a difference and can largely compensate for natural ability, they will be more inclined to work hard.

School staff must not only communicate to students that their efforts matter, but also genuinely believe it and develop policies and practices built on that belief. Faith in the value of hard work should play out daily in hundreds of small ways. Admission to advanced placement courses, for example, should not be strictly limited: if students want to commit to the work involved in an AP course, they should be encouraged to go for it. This encouragement should consist in part of identifying and addressing prerequisite skills that the students may lack, and letting them know that the course will require a sizeable investment of effort. At the same time, educators must communicate to their students their genuine confidence that, if they make the required effort, they will be successful.

We Believe: That Success Breeds Success

Successes are not isolated events; rather, they build on and reinforce one another. There is a circular relationship between success and self-confidence: when students succeed in school, they learn that they are capable of success, and are willing in turn to take on additional challenges. The reverse is also true: when students begin to fail, their school behavior becomes increasingly motivated by avoidance—they disappear into the back of the room or sink down into their chairs, hoping to hide. The last thing they want is to be called on. When confident students receive a graded paper covered with red marks pointing out errors, they study the comments to try to understand where they went wrong. Discouraged students, on the other hand, are much more likely to wad up the paper and throw it away. They are not inclined to learn from their mistakes or to profit from teacher feedback.

In the past, schools were apparently organized around the belief that students are motivated by the fear of failure; we now recognize that such a belief only reinforces an already poor self-concept. Fear of failure can only motivate students who have a pattern of success. Such students confront problems as soon as they run into them, and redouble their efforts to do better: "I'm not going to let *that* happen again," they think to themselves.

Less-confident students, on the other hand, tend to react with a shrug when they perform poorly: "Oh well, I never was very good at this."

One challenge for school staff is to increase the range of what students feel they are "good" at. The success orientation of the school and the staff's understanding that "success breeds success" are important tools in this respect. One daily practice based on this belief—and, of course, tailored to students of different ages—is to divide the curriculum into small enough "chunks" for students to see their progress on a frequent basis.

We Believe: That Adults Influence Student Confidence

Adults who are asked to recall memorable experiences from their school years will often identify teachers who significantly influenced them. Typically, they will say such things as "He really believed in me," or "I didn't think I could do algebra (or volleyball, or music), but she convinced me I could be good at it." Depending on the age of the speaker, these memories may have endured for 40 years or more.

It's important to recognize that the confidence teachers express in their students may contrast with the attitudes to which the students are exposed at home. Parents may be genuinely surprised when their children do well in school: they might believe, for example, that math skills are not part of their genes, or that girls aren't good at science, or that their family was never good at sports. Educators, then, have a particular responsibility to bolster student confidence and to help students overcome the ignorance or apathy that they might have to cope with at home. Educators typically act

upon this responsibility in very small ways, such as quiet conversations (suggesting, for example, that a student try out for choir or enroll in an advanced course).

We Believe: That Schools Control the Conditions of Success

Over the past 40 years or so, many educators came to believe that the primary determinant of students' success in school was the socioeconomic status of their parents, and the mother's education level in particular (Coleman, 1961). Educators and policymakers concluded that there was not much that schools could do to overcome such factors. Of course, students' lives and opportunities outside of school *do* affect their learning: children from homes that are rich in learning opportunities— where grammatical English is spoken, challenging questions are asked at the dinner table, and frequent trips are taken to interesting places—will find school learning far easier than will those whose parents speak little English, read infrequently if at all, and have their physical and intellectual horizons limited by poverty or ignorance.

Schools can, however, help students to surmount any negative influences they may encounter at home. Years of research, initially through the effective schools movement and continuing to this day, have demonstrated that students from impoverished or limited backgrounds fare much better in some schools than in others. Consequently, educators who used to ask of these students: "What can we expect?" must instead inquire: "What can we *do?*"

We Believe: That the Bell Curve Mentality Must Be Abandoned

The "bell curve" mentality has a grip on the belief structure of many schools, and is therefore worth exploring in some detail. The bell curve is based on a statistical phenomenon called "normal distribution," which reflects the distribution of randomly occurring events. Let's say, for example, that we had to measure the heights of the population of a town. Some of the people would be tall, a lot would be somewhere in the middle, and a few would be quite short. Their heights, in other words, would fall along a "normal" line of distribution. Because this distribution resembles a bell when plotted on a graph, it is sometimes referred to as a "bell curve" (Figure 2.1).

Now let's say we had to measure the heights of members of a basketball team. In this case, we can be sure that most of the people measured are tall. Our line of distribution, then, might feasibly look more like the boldface curve in Figure 2.2.

The bell curve is relevant to school improvement because it has proven to be fairly descriptive of student learning under certain conditions—namely, traditional instructional approaches and fixed amounts of time. When a pre-established time frame is allotted for a given topic (e.g., three weeks for fractions in math class), and when students are assigned to grade levels based on their ages alone, student learning tends to follow the bell curve pattern. Under these conditions, a few students will excel, many others will grasp some of the material, and a few others will not understand it at all.

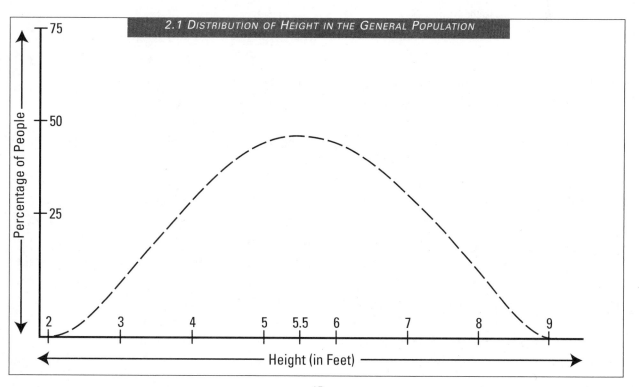

2.1 DISTRIBUTION OF HEIGHT IN THE GENERAL POPULATION

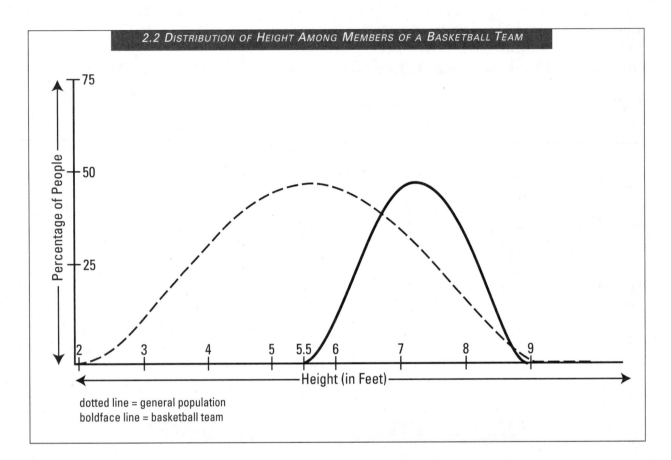

2.2 DISTRIBUTION OF HEIGHT AMONG MEMBERS OF A BASKETBALL TEAM

dotted line = general population
boldface line = basketball team

There is nothing inherently wrong with the bell curve; it merely illustrates the reality that, under conventional conditions, some students learn at high levels while others do poorly. The problem is that educators and the general public alike have come to see the bell curve as prescriptive rather than descriptive; many people now believe that it is natural and acceptable to apply the curve to student learning. Many educators believe it is inevitable that only a few students in each class will learn very well, and that a few students will just as inevitably fail. The bell curve belief is even institutionalized in the grading policies of some schools, where *A*'s are restricted to a

small number of students, and teachers are required to assign *C*'s to most of the others.

If the bell curve mentality is abolished in schools, and if schools are organized to promote high-level learning of all students, the consequences can be dramatic. It is possible that all students—even those from limited backgrounds— will have access to opportunities that their ancestors did not. This is, of course, the American dream: that education can provide a way to escape the cycle of ignorance and poverty. Nothing can be guaranteed, but a culture of success and high expectations is clearly essential to helping students do well at school and in later life.

We Believe: The Schools Must Cultivate a Culture of Respect

All people, regardless of age or role, deserve respect and should be treated with dignity. Students may be young, but they are every bit as human as the adults at school, and should be treated as such. Similarly, office and custodial staff—although regarded by many as playing a lesser role than teachers and administrators—are critical to helping carry out the school's mission and should thus also be accorded respect.

Some adults, even those who work in schools, forget the imperative to treat everyone well: they talk down to students, dismiss their accounts of situations, and cut them off when they are speaking. In some schools, even parents are treated without the courtesy due to adults in any setting; instead, they are assumed to be troublemakers or to represent problems of some kind. In fulfilling the truly stressful demands of their work, educators sometimes forget that their students are also working hard, and that parents are primarily interested in their children's learning. Schools are, after all, three-way partnerships among teachers, students, and parents; all parties to this important work must be treated with the presumption of positive intentions. Given the fact that some parents will have had negative experiences in school when they were younger, educators must make a special effort to reach out to them and make them feel welcome.

The belief that all people should be treated with respect can promote certain attitudes and behaviors if truly accepted and internalized by all. A school operating under this belief will not, for example, allow students, teachers, or parents to be kept waiting to see an administrator, particularly if they have an appointment or were summoned to the office. Policies regarding minor administrative details, such as using the copy machine, will reflect a similar attitude of trust toward teachers and students.

We Believe: That Schools Must Be Responsive to Their "Clients"

This belief reflects a commitment never to forget who the intended beneficiaries of school are: the students and, indirectly, their parents. Schools must be responsive to students and their parents and put their needs over the personal preferences of staff.

This focus on clients is, of course, central to the quality movement, and has had a powerful effect on corporations, nonprofit organizations, and government agencies. The philosophy, if not all the details, of the quality movement applies well to schools. Neither students nor parents should ever feel that schools are organized for the convenience of their employees, rather than for the maximum learning of the students. Administrative rules—for example, the procedures for course selection, before- or after-school clubs, and field trip permissions—should be reasonable and clear to both students and their parents; school staff should make every effort to be flexible, inclusive, and welcoming. A focus on clients suggests that the common practice of assigning the most preparations and the most challenging students to the newest and least-experienced teachers would stop. Experienced teachers do not "earn" the right to an easier teaching load, fewer preparations, and more high-level courses. A school committed to the learning of all students will assign the most experienced and skilled teachers to the students who most need their help, and encourage them to share their wisdom with newer colleagues.

Of course, focusing on clients means much more than making the school as convenient as possible for them. It touches all aspects of the operation. Public schools are institutions created by the community for the purpose of educating its children. They are also complex organizations, with many intersecting parts; consequently, it takes enormous determination for educators to ask of all the decisions they make: "How does this improve the learning of students?"

We Believe: That a Sense of Democracy Should Affect Decision Making

Some organizations are very top-down institutions, in which those at the top make all the important decisions and communicate them down the line. In schools, these decisions may affect student discipline and attendance policies, course offerings, school schedule, instructional teams, budgets, procedures for teacher evaluation and professional development, and the like. In schools with a top-down culture, teachers are not permitted to play an active role in their own performance appraisals—that job is restricted to administrators. Similar expectations prevail with respect to budgets and sundry other decisions. Students, likewise, are considered to be mere *consumers* of school policies rather than *producers*.

If a school is to be a true learning community, both teachers and students must have the opportunity to help develop policies and practices that

affect them. Of course, not every teacher wants to participate in endless discussions about, say, a revised discipline policy, but administrators should accommodate the expertise and perspective of every teacher when developing procedures. Similarly, students have important insights into how their peers perceive the school's approach to student conduct, and they can help shape a policy that commands student respect and acceptance. The same thinking should inform the school's approach to all-important decisions: those affected by a policy should have at least the opportunity to participate in its formulation.

Many schools have established formal decision-making procedures that permit the participation of students and staff, while other schools operate more on an ad hoc basis. Either way, these schools recognize that the door should always be open—decisions should not be made in "smoke-filled rooms" to which access is limited. At a school with democratic decision-making procedures in place, the student council would consider important decisions affecting student life and culture and make recommendations for faculty and administrative review, and professional development offerings would be designed by faculty, based on teacher self-assessment and goal setting or on the analysis of data that points to instructional improvements needed.

We Believe: That All Work Has Value and Dignity

In an era of increased stakes and accountability, it is a challenge to create schools that do not take an elitist attitude toward certain types of student goals. In the nation's most acclaimed public secondary schools, for example, a student who does not aim to attend a highly selective college may be made to feel inadequate ("Only the Ivy League is good enough for us!"). Of course, there are multiple paths to professional fulfillment. Working as a carpenter or photojournalist, managing a political campaign, running the lights in a theater production, and repairing automobiles are all challenging jobs that need not require a college degree. Students who are inclined toward such work must never be made to feel that they are somehow second-class citizens in school. The school culture should never assume that excellence is defined only as an abstract academic performance that yields high scores on the SAT or ACT and admission to a selective college: all work, when conducted with energy, commitment, and pride, is worthwhile. The school's obligation is to help each student find self-fulfillment and actualization, and to ensure that the culture of the school respects all lines of endeavor. Schools in which all types of work are considered worthy of respect will include opportunities for and recognition of student achievement in the subjects and projects that interest their students.

We Believe: That Competition Is Generally Damaging to Both Students and Teachers

In general, competition is a highly destructive force. Some competition is of course inevitable—such as in athletic events—and many secondary schools are required to produce a class rank of seniors for use in college admissions. In addition, some teachers would argue that a judicious use of competition can motivate students, encouraging them, for example, to study words for a spelling

bee, or to be the first to complete a timed math test. However, much competition has negative consequences, both for students individually and for the culture of the school as a whole. When students are pitted against one another, they learn to take pleasure in the misfortunes and missteps of others, rather than offering support and encouragement. Students who habitually find themselves on the lower rung of a competitive ladder will eventually succumb to low expectations for their own future performance, allowing past experiences to influence their self-confidence.

In general, the same principle applies to adults: teachers are highly sensitive to being compared with their colleagues and found wanting. Although a school committed to improvement must recognize excellence and establish procedures for sharing expertise, the school environment must be one of mutual support. Both teachers and administrators must ensure that the culture among adults promotes cooperation and collaboration rather than competition. Because some adult competition is nearly always under the surface, ensuring its elimination requires vigilance and sensitivity.

Educators who believe in the generally corrosive nature of competition will create some guidelines for its use, such as the following:

➤ Students should compete against themselves only. For example, when students time their performance on a test, they should compete against their own best time, not that of their classmates.

➤ Student work that is generally subject to competition, such as in a science fair, should be evaluated against external standards of quality, rather than against the work of other students. This implies that top awards should go to all projects that meet the standards, not only to the "best" entry.

➤ The adult culture in the school should be free of competition among individual teachers, teams, departments, and grade levels, as well as between novice and experienced teachers.

Summary

The beliefs held by a school's staff and its parent community are arguably the most important deter-minant of the culture, policies, and practices of a school, providing the backlight for everything that goes on there. Often, when school practices are held up to a school's stated beliefs, many are found to be in poor alignment, or even to be working at cross purposes. Beliefs, particularly unexamined ones, tend to be highly resistant to change, and can therefore constitute a serious drag on schools trying to achieve ambitious goals for student learning. It is essential that school leaders help staff and parents to explore the school's beliefs and their impact on the school program.

➤ ➤ ➤

3

What We Know

W hat we know" provides the research base for school practices; it offers a critical screen up to which educators can hold their ideas and gauge their likely effectiveness. If an approach has achieved good results in other places and circumstances, and with similar students, it is likely to help a school achieve its own goals. Conversely, a school would probably decide not to implement a practice for which the research literature has revealed poor results.

Educational research is, of course, vast; a search for information on any topic yields hundreds of articles. Although many of these represent small-scale studies with limited application to any particular location, in total they represent a huge body of knowledge. Because educational research is also continually evolving, findings must always be considered subject to revision. At a typical meeting of the American Educational Research Association, hundreds of papers are presented on a wide variety of topics. Again, many of these, taken alone, are of only limited value for any particular situation. But in total, and as summarized in meta-analyses, they can yield extremely valuable information for policy-makers and practitioners.

Challenges of Educational Research

All educational research presents practitioners with difficulties when they attempt to apply results to their own settings. These challenges, along with numerous questions for educators to ponder, are described briefly below.

Imprecise Measures of Effectiveness

The most common measure of the effectiveness of a given instructional practice is student scores on standardized tests. But is this good evidence? Do the tests actually measure what the instructional technique was meant to accomplish? If the method was intended to teach writing, or scientific investigation, or mathematical problem solving, would higher scores on a multiple-choice, machine-scorable test prove its efficacy? If research is based on more dependable measures, are there enough students in the sample to yield reliable results, and are those evaluating the student work adequately trained to make valid and consistent judgments?

Technical Problems

Is the data cross-sectional (e.g., comparing this year's 4th graders with last year's 4th graders) or longitudinal (comparing 4th grade scores from the end of this year with scores at the beginning of the year, or at the beginning of the students' 3rd grade year)? If the former, are the groups of 4th graders equivalent? If the latter, did any students move in or out of the class, and would those movements affect the assessment results?

Have the backgrounds of students been taken into account? Students are far from equal when it comes to their upbringing and their lives outside of school. Some families reinforce and extend their children's schoolwork, take them on trips during weekends and vacations, and provide them with a safe and secure environment at home; others are barely able to offer their children a quiet place to do their homework. These factors can greatly affect how much students learn in a year, and may well affect the results of studies designed to measure the impact of a certain instructional method. Educators should also consider whether or not the findings for a particular instructional method could be skewed by the effects of a concurrent intervention that researchers did not account for.

Despite these factors, practitioners can still learn from educational research, which—imperfect though it is—can help them to design their school programs. For the purposes of this book, I have clustered recent research findings into categories designed to yield the greatest benefit for educators seeking a comprehensive approach to school improvement. Because the literature on these subjects has been summarized in many books and articles, I present here only those elements that have the greatest potential to influence educational practice. Although educators must recognize the limitations of educational research and take any findings with a grain of salt, they also must distill the most useful results and apply them to their own settings.

Research on Learning

Arguably, the most critical body of research for educators to incorporate into their practice is that on learning—after all, promoting student learning is the essential mission of schools. Only by understanding how people—both children and adults—learn can educators hope to design instructional programs that will maximize that learning.

The Incredible Brain

The fields of neurology and cognitive psychology have fascinated researchers and educators since at least the early 20th century, and research on both topics has exploded since about 1980, fueled by sophisticated diagnostic tools and studies of animal learning and behavior.

Neurons. A child is born with approximately 100 billion neurons—the cells that, along with glial cells, compose the central nervous system. Although the number of neurons was believed for many years to be fixed at birth, there is recent evidence that new brain cells may actually be generated throughout a person's life (Gould, Reeves, Graziano, & Gross, 1999; Kempermann & Gage, 1999).

Brain Hemisphericity. The left and right sides of the brain control different aspects of thought and action, but they work together at all times. Therefore, rather than attempting to teach to the "left" or the "right" side of the brain, educators should teach to both (Ornstein, 1997).

The Brain as Information Processor. Most cognitive psychologists now believe that the brain processes information in three stages: sensory memory, working memory, and long-term memory. In the sensory memory stage, the brain scans all input and discards most of it as irrelevant; most learning occurs during working memory, and knowledge is stored in long-term memory. Much of what educators call "learning" occurs through the brain's pattern-seeking mechanism in the stage of working memory.

Memory. Some people may remember information by engaging in "rote rehearsal"—the repetition of the information over and over until it becomes automatic and can be accessed while the brain is engaged in other cognitive activities. Complex data, however, require active mental processing (e.g., creating appropriate metaphors and predicting outcomes), during which the brain engages with the information to make it meaningful. Students who need to learn information that is not immediately relevant, such as the elements of the periodic table, might memorize them using mnemonic devices. Furthermore, when individuals are emotionally engaged in a learning experience, the learning is far more likely to be permanent than when the emotions are not involved.

Learning as Mental Action

After analyzing data from more than 1,500 elementary, middle, and high schools in the United States, researchers at the Center on Organization and Restructuring of Schools at the University of Wisconsin-Madison discovered that students who participated in "authentic instruction"—in which they engaged in high-level understanding and application of information to the world beyond school—outscored their peers on traditional assessments. The study, conducted over five years, found that the most successful schools had teachers and administrators who formed a professional learning community focused on student work and performance, modified their instructional practice when necessary to get better results, and concentrated on four key factors: student learning, authentic pedagogy, school organizational capacity, and external support (Newmann & Wehlage, 1995).

According to research by the NTL Institute for Applied Learning (1998), learning and retention rates vary enormously according to the methods used. Students who learn through the lecture method retain about 5 percent of their lesson—10 percent when they read along with the lecture; audiovisual presentations increase the retention rate to 30 percent, and discussion groups to 50 percent. The most effective approaches—resulting in 75 percent and 90 percent retention rates, respectively—are learning by doing (such as through the inquiry method) and learning by teaching others.

Research on Teaching

In some respects, it is difficult to defend the distinction between research on learning and that on teaching. However, there are specific strategies—in addition to a general orientation toward teaching for understanding, or encouraging students to develop their own concepts—that can enhance student learning.

➤ According to the process-product researchers Brophy and Good (1986), the practices of effective teachers include careful lesson planning, articulation of learning goals to students, monitoring of student work, and use of time-on-task tactics.

➤ Fasko and Grubb (1995) found that effective teachers implement more learner-centered and active-learning practices—such as critical thinking, inquiry-based practices, and hands-on activities—than do less effective teachers.

➤ Marzano, Pickering, and Pollock (2001) have identified nine categories of research-based instructional strategies that improve student achievement:

o Identifying similarities and differences

o Summarizing and note taking

o Reinforcing effort and providing recognition

o Assigning homework

o Using nonlinguistic representations

o Fostering cooperative learning

o Setting objectives and providing feedback

o Generating and testing hypotheses and questions

o Providing cues and advance organizers

➤ Students obtained higher achievement scores and demonstrated significantly more positive attitudes toward a subject when evaluated using criterion-referenced methods (Wilburn & Felps, 1983). Effective teachers use assessment results not only to evaluate student work, but also to inform teaching methods—and as instructional tools in and of themselves (Pressley, Yokoi, Rankin, Wharton-McDonald, & Mistretta, 1997; Darling-Hammond, Ancess, & Falk, 1995).

➤ Teacher knowledge and skill level significantly affect student achievement (Darling-Hammond, 1997; Brophy, 1986). Because teachers regularly use their knowledge base when designing and assessing learning activities, student learning is limited by what the teacher knows (Goldhaber & Brewer, 1996).

Feedback to Students

"Feedback" here refers to information provided to students on their learning—usually by a teacher, but also by other students, or by the very design of an instructional activity.

➤ In order for feedback to affect student learning and self-confidence, it must be timely and unambiguous (Porter & Brophy, 1988).

➤ It is difficult for learners to gauge how they are doing without ongoing feedback (Corcoran & Wilson, 1989).

➤ Emmer (1988) determined that overenthusiastic praise for correct answers loses its effectiveness over time. Feedback must therefore be diagnostic in nature, and should always be constructive rather than destructive.

➤ Feedback is necessary to establish learning goals and improve achievement outcomes (Schunk, 1998).

Research on Motivation

What makes people do what they do? Why do some individuals work hard every day while others can't be bothered? Are people motivated by fear, intrinsic satisfaction, praise, money, or other rewards? Recent research sheds some light on the issue of motivation.

The Role of Expectations

Parents and educators have long recognized the role of expectations in shaping student behavior and commitment to learning. Indeed, expectations, both positive and negative, have a way of becoming self-fulfilling prophecies.

➤ Rosenthal and Jacobson (1968) found that low teacher expectations influenced student achievement.

➤ Many studies have found that student achievement is enhanced when teachers communicate high expectations to their students (Rutter, Maughan, Mortimore, & Ouston, 1979; Mortimore, 1991).

➤ Studies indicate that when certain students are identified as having performed poorly, regardless of whether they actually had or not, teachers form preconceptions of the students' future performance (Covington 1992; Marshall & Weinstein, 1984, 1987).

Extrinsic and Intrinsic Motivation

Extrinsic motivation, as its name suggests, is influenced by factors external to the learner, such as praise or material rewards. Intrinsic motivation, on the other hand, refers to the learner's own internal drive for achievement, fueled by the satisfaction of mastery or of a job well done.

➤ Brophy has argued that intrinsically motivated learning can take place only if students are cognitively ready to attempt a new task, and if the learning experience is relevant to the students' interests (cited in Johnson-Grooms, 1999).

➤ Helping students identify goals and connect their learning to those goals fosters intrinsic *and* extrinsic motivation (DeBacker & Nelson, 2000; Schunk, 1998).

➤ Keller (1983) has identified four major dimensions of effective classroom motivation: interest, relevance, expectancy of success, and satisfaction resulting from positive consequences of learning performance.

➤ Motivation is enhanced through reinforcement and positive feedback, and verbal praise can function as an extrinsic motivator (Kamins & Dweck, 1999; Kohn, 1993; Scheerens, 1992).

➤ Stringer and Hurt (1981) have suggested that when students are intrinsically motivated to perform a task, the task itself is rewarding. According to their study, the addition of extrinsic motivation to the task does not increase motivation. On the contrary, it may even cause a student to lose interest in the work.

Research on Attribution Theory

Attribution theory refers to the factors to which students assign their learning results. When students have a hard time learning or do poorly on a test, to what do they attribute that difficulty?

➤ Dweck demonstrated that learners' beliefs about their own intelligence influence their learning (1986).

➤ Attributing success and failure to different factors results in different consequences for learners: students who attribute their poor results to lack of ability or effort on their part tend to become less motivated to learn than do those who blame external factors beyond their control, such as poor teaching or lack of access to books (Atkinson, 1975).

➤ Dweck, Goetz, and Strauss (1980) have found that women are more likely than men to attribute failure to a lack of ability, making them likelier to anticipate further failure. According to Dweck and Repucci (1973), boys tend to attribute failure either to a lack of effort or to bad luck.

➤ Among older elementary students, levels of confidence depend largely on whether the students believe intelligence to be fixed or malleable (Cain & Dweck, 1995).

➤ Stevenson (1990) found that when asked to explain differences in student achievement, Japanese teachers tended to cite "hard work"

whereas American teachers cited "student ability." In other words, American teachers attribute student performance to *who the students are,* and Japanese teachers attribute it to *what students do.* (Neither Japanese nor American teachers attributed student learning to their own instructional skills.)

Research on Leadership

School leadership requires the capability to develop, communicate, and put into place a vision for school improvement that marshals the energies of disparate members of a staff around common goals. Visionary leadership enables staff members to regard the most mundane aspects of their roles in light of their relation to promoting student learning. Although largely considered the province of the administration, leadership may be exercised by anyone in the school: true leaders can include teachers, or even the school secretary.

➤ All members of the school staff are responsible for helping students learn because they share a belief that all students possess the capacity to learn (Rosenholtz, 1985; Edmonds, 1984).

➤ Nanus (1992) has argued that vision is the key to effective leadership.

➤ According to Corcoran, Fuhrman, and Belcher (2001), developing school capacity requires strong leadership.

➤ Administrators will improve school performance by maintaining a focus on core instruction as well as on other aspects of the school program, such as scheduling, grading, grouping of students, and establishing a sense of community within the school (Newmann,

Rutter, & Smith, 1989).

➤ Cohen, Raudenbush, and Loewenberg-Ball (2000) have pointed out that "Coordinating teaching and learning is less difficult in environments with coherent organization and guidance for instruction, and more difficult in those that lack such coherence" (p. 13).

➤ Unfortunately, consensus, collaboration, and cooperation between teachers and administrators are rarely found in schools (Barth, 1990).

➤ When administrators don't understand the nuances of school-improvement efforts, effective instructional practices, and professional community building, school reform efforts fail (Conti, Ellsasser, & Griffin, 2000).

➤ Principals should provide continuous visible support and reorganize school resources such as time, staff, and money to enable learning by all (Wilson & Corbett, 1999; Wohlestetter, Mohrman & Robertson, 1997; Mizell, 1994).

➤ Encouraging teachers to collect, organize, and evaluate school and classroom data to inform their practice can help improve a school (Senese, 2000; King, 1999).

➤ Administrators should eliminate such "hazing" practices as assigning the least experienced teachers to the toughest classes, or rewarding the most experienced teachers with the most advanced students and the fewest preparations. (Darling-Hammond, 1997).

➤ Teachers who use their knowledge to solve school problems collaboratively tend to be particularly satisfied with and committed to their jobs. Reflection, dialogue, and inquiry can enhance teachers' collaborative efforts by helping them identify and resolve common challenges. Teachers who work collaboratively with peers, administrators, parents, and community members are better able to transform practice and thereby improve both their professional practice and student learning (Stigler & Hiebert, 1999).

➤ According to Fullan (2000), teachers demonstrate leadership by developing practices that move away from undesirable norms, such as teaching in isolation and teaching as technical work.

➤ Teachers' roles must be developed in a way that changes the internal conditions of schools to better deal with problems associated with teaching and learning (Conti, Ellsasser, & Griffin, 2000).

Research on School Organization

The various components of school organization are generally regarded as the most impervious to change, since they deal with the very heart of how the school operates: the schedule, the departments or teams, the number of students assigned to a class. However, these are matters over which a school's staff has some influence, and research has addressed most of them.

School Size

➤ There is very little agreement about what constitutes small or large schools. According to a review by Cotton (2001) of the literature on school size, the definition of a small school varies widely.

➤ Raywind (1998) studied 103 documents related to school size, none of which found larger schools to be advantageous; small schools, on the other hand, *have* been proven to be more conducive to academic achievement (Eichenstein, 1994; Bates, 1993; Walberg, 1992).

➤ Small schools have been found to increase student achievement for students of low socioeconomic status as well as for minority students (Kershaw & Blank, 1993; Stockard & Mayberry, 1992).

➤ Small schools report better attendance and fewer discipline problems than larger ones, and are more cost effective (Howley, 1996; Burke, 1987).

➤ The ability to provide learning opportunities and create a culture that supports learning is enhanced when schools are organized into small learning communities (McPartland, Balfanz, Jordan, & Legters, 1998; Galletti, 1998).

➤ According to Cawelti (1993), research on the effects of schools-within-a-school (SWAS) is still limited and therefore inconclusive. Some researchers, however, have found that SWAS are not as effective as small schools, and that a small school should exist as its own entity rather than within a large school in order to be effective (Howley, 1996; Meier, 1995).

Class Size

➤ The Tennessee class size experiment demonstrated that students learn better when class sizes are reduced (Mosteller, 1995; Finn & Achilles, 1990).

➤ Achilles (1997) has shown that a ratio of 15 students per class, especially in the 1st grade, has the greatest effect on student achievement. Among other things, small classes encourage more positive engagement by students.

➤ Farber and Finn (2000) found that 4th graders who had experienced small classes through the 3rd grade were more engaged in learning than those who had experienced full-size classes with teacher aides. However, slight changes in class size, such as from 27 to 22 students, have only a minor effect on student achievement.

Grouping for Instruction

Tracking—the practice of separating students into different academic programs according to their perceived abilities and prospects—tends to relegate many students, typically poor and minority children, to a less challenging curriculum and less qualified teachers.

➤ Research on permanent tracks has shown that those in "lower" tracks learn less than their peers (Gamoran et al., 1997).

➤ Although virtually no researchers argue in favor of tracking, particularly when it leads to discrimination by class, race, or gender, many teachers and parents support the practice (White et al., 1996).

➤ The research on flexible instructional groups is more encouraging than that on tracking: evidence indicates that grouping can increase student achievement and allow for remediation or enrichment when necessary (Slavin, 1987).

➤ Lou, Abrami, and Spence (2000) found small-group instruction to have a small but significantly positive effect on student achievement.

➤ According to Wynne and Walberg (1994), small groups exert a powerful emotional influence on members.

➤ Grouping schemes must be properly implemented if they are to succeed: study after study indicates that cooperative learning is ineffective unless properly implemented (Johnson & Johnson, 1999).

➤ Students who are taught how to cooperate within a group demonstrated better reading comprehension (Battistich et al., 1993), mathematical problem solving (Leikin & Zaslavsky, 1997; Nichols & Hall, 1995), and conceptual understanding of science (Balkcom, 1992).

➤ Cooperative learning can produce desired learning outcomes and promotes social acceptance and positive student interactions (Johnson et al., 1981).

Scheduling

As Canady and Rettig (2000) have noted, "A school schedule can have an enormous impact on a school's instructional climate" (p. 375). Some schools have implemented alternatives to the traditional schedule, of which block scheduling is the most prominent; because it creates longer blocks of time for each class, many think block scheduling permits greater teacher and student concentration on complex content. Block scheduling also provides students with increased off-campus learning opportunities at local universities or businesses. The research evidence on block scheduling is mixed. This may be due in part to the different applications and definitions of the practice, such as the A/B, four-by-four, and parallel (PBS) models (Canady & Rettig, 2001).

➤ Some 100 case studies, along with the extensive work of Canady and Rettig, have shown that block scheduling allows middle- and high-school students to take more classes over the course of a year, making it easier for them to meet more stringent graduation requirements (Viadero, 2001).

➤ Proponents of block scheduling contend that it increases student achievement while also having a positive effect on attendance, dropout rates, discipline problems, tracking, remediation, and interactive learning (Queen & Isenhour, 1998; Canady & Rettig, 1995; Gunter, Estes, & Schwab, 1990).

➤ In elementary schools, the popular PBS configuration is designed around half-class instructional groups in reading and math. Although homerooms may have as many as 25 students, reading and math groups are typically restricted to fewer than 15—a number rarely reached by most class-size reduction initiatives, according to Achilles (1997).

➤ Many studies have found that block scheduling and other scheduling options benefit some at-risk students, who achieve at higher levels when allowed to take fewer courses on a more intensive basis (Framer, 1997; Carroll, 1994; Fletcher, 1997).

➤ On the other hand, York (1997) concluded that block scheduling doesn't have any effect on student achievement, and Queen (2000) has found the differences between block and traditional scheduling to be negligible. Several Canadian researchers report that block scheduling actually has a negative effect on students (Viadero, 2001).

➤ Queen (2000) has found that appropriate changes to instructional practices and effective use of class time are critical to any scheduling initiatives, especially in the case of block scheduling.

➤ Teachers need to increase their repertoire of teaching strategies if any scheduling configuration that maximizes student-learning time is to be effective (Queen, Algozzine, & Eaddy, 1997).

➤ Studies suggest that teachers must use instructional time wisely and develop various instructional strategies to engage students in learning (Skrobarcek., 1997).

Research on Family Involvement

Educators have long recognized the importance of establishing and maintaining links with the families of their students. The effectiveness of these efforts is borne out in the research.

➤ Effective schools seek out relationships with parents and the community (Fullan, 2000); Finn (1998) argues that schools must foster programs and develop school cultures that encourage parental involvement.

➤ Students learn more when parents are actively involved in their education—when parents read to them, limit their television viewing, supervise how they spend their time, and take an interest in their progress at school (Horn & Chen, 1998; Keith & Keith, 1993; Shartrand et al., 1997; 1995).

➤ School practices that respect the cultural and family backgrounds of their students can increase and enhance partnerships between home and school. According to Epstein and Connors (1994), researchers at the Johns Hopkins University Center on Families, Communities, Schools, and Children's Learning concluded that the following six activities promote parental involvement at school and at home:

- o Parent education
- o Communication between the school and home
- o Volunteering
- o Learning at home
- o Shared decision making
- o Collaboration with the community

Summary

Many years ago, Madeline Hunter pointed out the difference in how education and other professions (notably medicine) apply the findings of research to their practices (1982). In the medical profession, the average time that elapses between a conclusive finding and its widespread application is five years; in education, the comparable number is 50 years. There are many explanations for this phenomenon, including the highly political nature of schools and school governance. However, any profession worthy of the name must ensure that its practices are supported by current research, and that its practitioners are prepared to change their practices as the research evolves.

➤ ➤ ➤

4

What We Do

It is in the decisions about what we do, of course, that "the rubber hits the road." When determining particular courses of action, educators draw on their beliefs and knowledge in light of what they are trying to achieve; any practices put in place must support the school's goals (*what we want*) while reflecting its underlying values (*what we believe*) and relevant research (*what we know*).

There is an especially close relationship between what we do and what we believe. We know that beliefs influence actions; but can actions also influence beliefs? There is considerable evidence that they can. For example, some teachers might believe, deep down and perhaps even subconsciously, that poor or minority students are incapable of higher-order analysis; when these students have difficulty with challenging concepts, such teachers might accept their struggle as reflective of "the way the world works" instead of aggressively helping the students master the material.

Now let's say these same teachers worked at a school that expects them to *behave as though* all students—girls as well as boys, black and white, rich and poor—are capable of higher-order thinking. In this case, they might arrange for extra help when poor or minority students encounter difficulty, or search for another approach, or enlist the assistance of an older student who understands the concept. In other words, the teacher would persevere. And when the struggling students finally succeed, the teachers might revise their beliefs about the "natural abilities" of certain students, particularly if faced with a number of similar cases. It is difficult, in other words, to sustain beliefs in the face of evidence to the contrary.

In a school committed to enhancing student learning, educators must examine all aspects of what they do to determine where best to invest their energy. The decisions teachers and administrators make every day must focus on improving student learning based on what we know and believe. Because practitioners are busy people, and because schools are complicated places with many interacting components, educators must set priorities among competing goals.

There are many different aspects of what we do, and although I discuss them individually in this chapter, they are highly intertwined. After all, schools are complex systems; the actions and structures of one part of a school bear directly on the others. For example, the way a school organizes its curriculum—whether it is integrated across disciplines, for instance—may affect the manner in which students are grouped, as well as the length of classes. Every category of what we do can be improved to enhance student achievement.

School improvement is a major undertaking, requiring serious and detailed planning: it should not be conducted in a hurry, with unrealistic deadlines or expectations. More importantly, though, school improvement represents *a way of thinking* about the work of education, and assumes educators to be flexible, goal-driven, and focused uncompromisingly on the mission of student learning and success. To use a cliché, school improvement is a process, not an event; it must become a way of life for the educators involved.

In order to embark on school improvement—to examine and revise what they do in schools in light of what they want, believe, and know—edu-

cators may need a roadmap, which I provide in this book. The framework consists of three fundamental parts: the Four Circles Model, policies, and programs. When these elements are aligned, the result is improved student learning—the bull's eye of the diagram. I have outlined the various components of my framework in this chapter, and they are described in greater detail in chapters 5–13.

Part 1: The Four Circles Model

The foundation of any approach to school improvement rests on the initial three circles of the Four Circles Model discussed in the preceding chapters: what we want, believe, and know. Resting on this foundation are specific school policies and organizational structures. These are schoolwide matters—such as the master schedule or the school's attendance policy—that affect the culture of the entire school, and as such constitute the context within which the school operates.

Most schools do not begin from scratch; their staffs inherit policies and structures that are already in place, and that may not have been altered in years, or even decades. These arrangements might therefore be perceived as "natural" or inevitable: the seven-period day, for example, or the teacher evaluation system might have been around so long as to be considered integral to the school.

In fact, of course, anything about a school may be changed to better educate students. But institutional change is not easy to accomplish, particularly when overhauling policies or structures that are deeply entrenched in the collective understanding of the place. Because some of a school's arrangements might be considered part of the school's identity, they may be highly resistant to change. Therefore, educators must recognize that changes in organizational structure may require considerable time to effect.

Part 2, Section 1: Policies

School Organization

School organization concerns the deployment of resources (i.e., space, time, people) within the school. Issues include the following:

➤ **The division of the school into departments, houses, or teams.** What are the sub groups within the school, if any? Are there schools-within-a-school? Do the 4th grade teachers work as a team, or is each a member of a multigrade "family" team? Is a large middle school divided into houses, and if so, do the houses correspond to different grades, or is each house made up of students from every grade? Are there smaller communities within high schools?

➤ **The master schedule.** How is time allocated? Although scheduling is handled differently in elementary, middle, and high schools, certain questions can be asked at all levels: How large are the blocks of instructional time? To what extent do teachers, possibly working within teams or houses, decide how to apportion their time among different activities? Are these allocations consistent across the entire school? In a high school, is the day divided into seven periods, or into two enormous blocks? In an elementary school, does the "specialist" schedule—that is, the time when music, art, and physical education teachers are available—determine the rest of the school schedule?

➤ **Allocation of space.** How are students and teachers assigned to space in the school? Is it possible to situate teams or houses adjacent to one another? (Teams may actually be created *because* of space restrictions.) Which classrooms are nearest to the library? Is there a learning support center, and if so, where is it located? Some of these decisions are essentially arbitrary, but others are more purposeful, and can further the goals of the school.

Policies and Practices Regarding Students

Much of a school's culture is a function of the policies and practices regarding students; they reflect, for example, the school's commitment to treating students with dignity and respect and putting a "success orientation" into place. These policies and practices are tremendously important to students, and largely define their school experiences. If policies are nonresponsive, punitive, or unfair, students will develop a negative feeling toward the school overall.

Among the policies and practices affecting students are the following:

➤ **A culture for learning.** Some schools have a positive culture regarding learning, perceiving it as important, fun, and worthwhile. In other schools, students are not committed to their studies, project the attitude that they are merely putting in time, and effect a nonchalant manner. These attitudes tend to be more pronounced at the secondary level, although they have their roots in elementary school. The prevailing culture in a school greatly influences student attitudes toward learning. What skills and talents are recognized? What is the balance between academics and athletics? Do students have the sense that they can succeed academically if they work hard, or are recognition and success reserved for only a small elite?

➤ **Discipline and attendance policies.** These help set the tone for a school, and to a large extent determine how students are treated on a day-to-day basis, by both teachers and office staff. Discipline and attendance policies also constitute the first substantive contact that many parents have with a school, as when they are called in regarding their child's misbehavior. In these instances, how are parents treated? What attitude does the staff convey with respect to the child? Do parents feel there is a presumption of innocence, or of guilt? Are attendance and discipline policies clearly articulated and unambiguous? Do they feel punitive to students? Are they rigid or flexible? Have they been affected by the "zero tolerance" philosophy? How are they formulated? Are students involved in their development?

➤ **Homework and grading policies.** Whereas discipline and attendance policies determine how students are treated in school as *people,* homework and grading policies affect how they are treated as *students.* These policies consist of schoolwide or individual teacher rules regarding homework completion, missed deadlines, and the determination of grades.

A school's approach to these matters, and particularly its grading policies, conveys much about its values. Educators must recognize at the outset the significant influence of these policies on the general tone and culture of the school. For example, a school communicates its expectations for student learning largely through its approach to grading: a bell curve policy suggests to students that only a few of them deserve high grades, regardless of how much they have learned. Educators should carefully examine school policies to ensure that they are sending the right signals to students and their parents.

Most schools that are committed to student learning allow students to participate in the formulation of policies and practices. Although virtually all schools have some type of student government in place, many of these don't represent genuine vehicles for student involvement; often they are essentially run by faculty advisors, and student participation is limited to minor matters, rubber-stamping, or fundraising drives.

Policies and Practices Regarding Staff

Schools have distinct cultures for both students and staff, either of which can be positive or negative, respectful or disrespectful. A negative staff culture, in which teachers and other staff members feel that their opinions don't matter and that they are treated in a punitive or disrespectful manner, can poison an entire school.

Aspects of a school's policies and organizational structures affecting staff must be designed with students in mind: it is not sufficient for a school to be comfortable for adults if it does not meet its goal of supporting high-level student learning. Educators must therefore keep one eye firmly fixed on the school's goals when determining staff policies and practices. Though I discuss these policies and practices in greater detail in Chapter 7, they include the following:

➤ **Decision making and budgeting.** How are decisions made in the school? How are the budgetary implications of these decisions sorted out? Is the school organized into teams, where one individual from each team—perhaps the team leader—also participates on the school council and reports back to the team, with recommendations for action? Are budgets developed in the same way? Does every member of the staff have an opportunity to participate, even at a distance, in budget decisions? When a small number of individuals make the decisions in a school—particularly those involving money—using a hidden process, the effect on the rest of the staff can be highly corrosive. Teachers must feel that decisions affecting their professional lives are transparent, and that they can contribute to them. The relationship between decisions and allocation of funds to the goal of student learning must be made absolutely clear; there is no place for favoritism and pet projects.

➤ **Professional development programs.** Successful schools take professional development seriously; they don't assume that initial levels of preparation will sustain teachers throughout their careers. An emphasis on professional development does not suggest that the quality of instruction is inadequate and must be "fixed," but rather reflects the difficulty and complexity of teaching and acknowledges that it is impossible to teach perfectly. Teaching can always be improved, and a school that is truly committed to student learning should never become complacent about teacher skills. Professional development has been transformed in recent years: in most schools, one-shot workshops have been replaced by more "job-embedded" approaches,

in which teachers engage in activities such as action research, collaborative work with colleagues, and reflective conversation. In addition, schools are recognizing the value of professional activities such as mentoring, serving on curriculum committees, and analyzing and assessing student work.

➤ **Teacher evaluation systems.** One of the most significant influences on a school's culture is its system for teacher evaluation, which must convey expectations for performance while simultaneously promoting professional learning. Such a system, focusing on both quality assurance and professional growth, is a challenge to design. As a general rule, an evaluation system must be based on clear and agreed-upon expectations for teaching while allowing teachers to play an active role in a fair, evidence-driven evaluation process that includes substantive and timely feedback. Such a system will lead to significant professional learning for teachers as well as to the quality assurance that every school must have. (I address this issue more fully in my 2000 book *Teacher Evaluation to Enhance Professional Practice*, cowritten with Tom McGreal.)

Linkages Beyond the School

Successful schools recognize that they exist within larger communities and actively cultivate outside relationships to promote school goals. I discuss this matter more fully in Chapter 8, but issues include the following:

➤ **Communication and partnership with parents.** Parents are not only their children's first teachers; they are essential school clients and partners of educators. Parents have insights about their children that can be of substantial value to teachers as they design learning experiences. Similarly, teachers see students in a different environment than do their parents, and can contribute to parent understanding of their children. Educators have a responsibility to keep parents informed about the instructional program and about the progress of their children, and parents can contribute to the conversation about the school's program and goals; parents can play an active role in encouraging their children to engage in learning and make connections between school learning and life outside of school.

➤ **Resources to support the instructional program.** These include outside speakers as well as settings for out-of-school learning, such as museums, factories, community agencies and services, and zoos. Learning can be greatly enhanced by excursions beyond the school's doors and enriched by visits from outside experts.

➤ **Coordination with community agencies for convenience and increased efficiency.** Many communities have found that they may extend public funds by situating a public library, for example, in a school. Such coordination eliminates the need for two separate facilities, and allows a single staff to serve both school and library clients; the joint library may also be open for longer hours than is typically possible for a library serving the school alone.

➤ **Relationships with businesses for both students and teachers.** Many business leaders are eager to incorporate students and teachers into their operations. These experiences are enriching for everybody: students get an

opportunity to see their studies applied to "the real world"; teachers, particularly those in the sciences, can use internships to keep their content knowledge sharp through interaction with professionals in the field; and those working in industry can find it refreshing to interact with school faculty and students.

➤ **Opportunities for service learning within the community.** Indications from many schools confirm the powerful influence that service learning can have on students' sense of efficacy and the development of caring for others. The most successful service-learning programs appear to be those in which students and agency workers are able to develop relationships: by returning to the same retirement home each year, for instance, students become familiar with its residents and their routines; this familiarity promotes caring and concern.

Part 2, Section 2: Programs

The next aspect of the school's structure concerns organization to support instruction. This level of planning is closest to the instructional work of teachers, and directly influences teacher effectiveness. Educators make hundreds of decisions daily that are heavily affected by schoolwide (or even district) decisions related to the following issues:

➤ **Aligned curriculum.** What are the goals for student learning in a particular course or year? The articulation of curriculum allows the school to translate its goals for student learning into specific guidance for teachers.

➤ **Assessment.** Do teachers create their own assessments? Do all teachers of a certain level or course administer the same assessments? Are the assessments of high quality? Are state or district assessments in place? Ideally, assessments should be developed by groups of teachers and used consistently, and can serve as the "operational definition" of the school's curriculum. Formative assessments may be used to provide feedback to students. In addition, when students are actively involved in self-assessment and monitoring of their learning, they are able to assume a genuine role in their own education.

➤ **Team planning.** Do teachers work independently, or together in instructional teams? Does the school use traditional scheduling or longer blocks of time? Are students tracked or grouped by skill level for any classes? Must students demonstrate proficiency in one subject before being eligible to participate in another? For example, is mastery of fractions and integers a prerequisite for Algebra I?

➤ **Learning support.** What type of support, paid for by categorical funds or allocated by the district, is available to help struggling students? Are there instructional aids? Is there a learning center? Is help available before or after school? The learning support system is the "safety valve" for student learning within the school, providing both teachers and students with the backup necessary to ensure successful learning.

Teaching

Classroom teaching is the complex work teachers do when interacting with students to engage them with the content and ensure that they learn it successfully. Naturally, successful teaching depends on other systems in the school: a clear curriculum, students with the necessary skills to be successful, and support for those who need additional assistance.

I discuss the framework for teaching offered here in greater detail in my book *Enhancing Professional Practice: A Framework for Teaching* (1996). The framework offers teachers, teacher preparation programs, and schools with the tools to engage in professional conversations about good teaching, and to analyze practice to determine how it can be improved. The framework is grounded in the concept of teaching as a complex cognitive activity; after all, teachers make hundreds of decisions daily about matters that directly affect student learning. It is also grounded in research on teaching and learning, and has been validated for teachers at all levels and years of experience. The framework divides teaching into four principal domains, which I describe in greater depth in Chapter 13:

➤ **Domain 1: Planning and Preparation.** Organizing the content to engage students in learning.

➤ **Domain 2: The Classroom Environment.** Establishing a culture for learning, and a respectful and safe learning atmosphere.

➤ **Domain 3: Instruction.** Engaging students actively in understanding the content of the curriculum.

➤ **Domain 4: Professional Responsibilities.** Activities beyond the classroom that maintain and advance the profession.

Because teaching can be defined as "that which causes learning," it is impossible to have successful instruction without successful learning. Good teaching, therefore, will include a success orientation on the part of teachers, together with specific actions to ensure learning. Sometimes this implies providing additional assistance to students, or seeking out other resources within or outside the school. Instruction, in other words, is the top of a conceptual framework, supported by all the other systems within the school and by the school's belief structure, and consistent with current research.

Summary

What we do is the heart of the school improvement effort, and requires serious effort on the part of educators. The different components of the school's program must be aligned not only with one another, but also with the school's articulated goals, its belief structure, and current research findings. Because of the complexity of this effort, and because the different components are so intertwined, a systematic approach is necessary. The framework and model I offer in this book can help guide educators through this complicated territory and focus their school-improvement efforts.

➤ ➤ ➤

Part 2:

The Framework for School Improvement

Once educators have agreed on what they want, believe, and know, they must examine the established policies and programs at their school and determine whether or not they should be reconsidered. To do so, both teachers and administrators should carefully evaluate whether or not the status quo is aligned with their goals and values and based on current research. Chapters 5–13 offer educators guidelines for assessing school and district procedures. In addition, each chapter includes a rubric summarizing the criteria for each of three levels of performance: poor, basic, and exemplary.

Policies

School
  Organization

Policies and Practices
  Affecting Staff

Policies and Practices
  Affecting Students

Linkages Beyond
  the School

5

School
Organization

"School organization" refers to how schools arrange the resources of time, space, and personnel for maximum effect on student learning. The school's organizational plan addresses those issues that affect the school as a whole, such as the master schedule, the location of staff in different rooms, and the assignment of aides to teachers or teams. (Matters that affect only individual teachers or teams—how to form reading groups for all 2nd graders, for example—are addressed in Chapter 11: Team Planning.)

Relationship to the Framework

How a school is organized is a matter for the staff to determine, and a school's organization should reflect the staff's commitment to the success of all students. Every aspect of the instructional program will convey the values and goals of the staff toward students and their learning.

High-Level Learning for All Students

Through a school's organizational patterns—whether the school is divided into teams or houses, for example, or whether it adopts a traditional or a block schedule—the staff can convey to both students and their parents that learning is important, that the business of the school is learning, and that the different elements of the school's organization are structured to support that learning. The master schedule, for example, is not established

43

merely for the convenience of the transportation department, although bus schedules are important and must be accommodated. Nor are teams established only so that members of the faculty who are friends can work together. All arrangements must reflect an unwavering focus on student learning.

A Safe and Positive Environment

The wise deployment of space can go a long way toward ensuring a physically safe environment, particularly for young children. If classrooms, the art room, restrooms, and the library are all within easy walking distance, and if the paths to each are safe, children will feel secure going alone. In addition, a school's arrangement of teachers into teams, houses, and the like can contribute to a feeling of community, and therefore emotional safety, for students; they should feel part of a group small enough that their absence or illness would be noticed.

A Culture of Hard Work and Opportunities for Success

A focus on success is not a matter of spoon-feeding. A good school organization will offer students the optimal degree of challenge, stretching them while at the same time ensuring that they can succeed if they exert the necessary effort. Students need to know (and may need to be reminded) that it is up to them to exert the effort. For example, elementary-school teachers might let their students know that they are free to go to the computer lab or learning center once they've completed their work and mastered certain tasks; similarly, students in middle or high school could be told that if they are willing to commit to a heavy workload and fill any gaps in their understanding,

they can enroll in Spanish II or an advanced placement course. Such opportunities should not constitute an exclusive club, open only to a few students; they should be open to any students willing to commit to them. The master schedule must be arranged to permit students to make these commitments and demonstrate their desire to participate in the most challenging opportunities the school has to offer.

When a school adopts a success orientation, it also commits itself to a flexible deployment of resources: nothing is carved in stone, and no one adopts a "take it or leave it" attitude. Students are assumed to be capable learners, and the school accepts its obligation to ensure successful learning by all students. Students should be able to get additional help when they need it, and to challenge the curriculum when they so choose; they should not be obliged to sit through a year of algebra if they can demonstrate, through a valid assessment, that they already understand the content. On the other hand, a student struggling with how to write a clear paragraph, for example, should be able to get help as needed.

School Organization

The research on school organization is clear: in general, small schools yield better results than large ones. This suggests that educators at large schools can help more students learn by creating subunits—schools within a school. Moreover, studies on teacher collaboration and teaming have shown that students benefit when teachers work together to promote student learning. Some schools in rural areas, of course, are *too* small, unable to provide a reasonable range of curricular or extracurricular offerings. But while educators in large schools can generally devise ways to break up into smaller units, those in small schools can't usually do much about their limited resources (although the Internet now provides students with learning opportunities that were not previously available).

Components of School Organization

Of course, most school staffs inherit a pre-existing organizational structure. For many educators, certain aspects of the school's organization—such as the number of classes in the master schedule in a high school or the houses in a middle school—are part of the school's very identity. This reality can make altering the school's organization slow and difficult. Still, educators should consider the following aspects of the school to determine which ones, if any, should be changed.

At the elementary-school level, units are usually instructional teams or grade-level groups, in which teachers work with students from classes other than their own homerooms. For example, three 4th grade teachers might choose to work together to teach all 100 children in the grade. Many middle schools have houses in place, which might be led for instance by four teachers, each representing core curricular areas, working together with a group of 100–125 students. (When these are multi-age groups and students remain with the same teachers over several years, teachers and students grow to know one another particularly well.) Many high schools establish schools-within-a-school to create smaller and more personal learning communities. Some of these are grade-based, whereas others are organized around an instructional focus, such as technology or the arts.

Master Schedule

The influence of the master schedule is hard to overstate. The schedule structures the pace of the interactions between students and teachers, and class length affects the nature of instruction and the depth to which students are able to go at any given time. At the elementary- and middle-school levels, the master schedule conveys the relative importance of different areas of study: for example, when language arts are allocated 90 minutes a day, and science is allocated 30 minutes twice a *week*, students and teachers receive powerful messages about the supposed value of each subject.

Alternatives to traditional scheduling practices at the middle- and high-school levels have been widely discussed in the educational literature under the general heading of "block scheduling." Although not a panacea, block scheduling can materially affect the quality of student-teacher interactions and the nature of teacher collaboration. The main characteristic of these approaches is that they organize instructional time into longer blocks than the traditional pattern, thus allowing teachers and students greater flexibility in how they use their time. With longer blocks of time, students can embark on projects that would be difficult to complete in only 43 minutes. Teachers accustomed to relying on lecturing find that they need to vary their approach under block scheduling, enabling students to engage in deeper and more sustained exploration of content.

Deployment of Instructional Personnel

Most elementary schools assign classroom teachers groups of 20–30 students, although there are usually other teachers available as well: specialists for subjects such as art, music, and physical education; state-funded remedial reading or math teachers; Title I teachers; and teachers funded through district or external funds to serve migrant students, ESL learners, or "gifted" students. In fact, some elementary schools have more "extra" teachers than they do regular ones! The situation is different at the middle- and high-school levels, where students rotate among content specialists. In schools committed to enhancing student learning, teachers go to considerable effort to integrate "special" subjects with more "academic" disciplines. Even when the schedule demands that a class of 3rd grade students goes to art class at, say, 11:00 a.m. on Thursdays, the art teacher and the homeroom teacher work to ensure that what the students are learning in the two classes is not completely separate.

Many schools—particularly at the elementary level, and sometimes motivated by state statute or by the promise of additional funds—have created more classes with fewer students in each. These efforts have had mixed results, partly because when overall class sizes are reduced, other expenses are inevitably increased—for more classroom space and for additional content specialists (and the classroom space that *they* need). In addition, there are frequently not enough qualified teachers to teach the new classes, especially at very large schools, resulting in at least a short-term reduction in teaching quality.

Although the research on class size has been inconclusive, studies suggest that reductions in size don't have much of an effect on student achievement unless the classes consist of 15 students or fewer. In any case, it is not the size of the

homerooms that matters, but the size of instructional groups; consequently, if the entire teaching staff can be deployed in a manner that greatly reduces the size of instructional groups, results are likely to improve. A school organizational structure that supports the use of *all* teaching staff (including those paid for by categorical funds) to provide basic instruction can result in much smaller instructional groups than are traditionally found in schools. (For more on this subject, see Chapter 12: Learning Support.)

Grouping Strategies

A school aiming to improve student performance must develop a reasoned approach, even a philosophy, toward the grouping of students for instruction. Such an approach should not include permanent tracking. When elementary-school students are clustered as "bluebirds" or "canaries" according to their real or perceived abilities, the groups often become permanent: those who are identified early on as particularly able tend to be the ones permitted to enroll in advanced courses in high school.

Permanent tracking harms all but the highest-performing students, who themselves gain only slightly from the practice. Short-term skill grouping, however, can be highly beneficial for all students. Students who do not understand, say, subtraction with regrouping should receive targeted instruction on the concept before moving on to a skill that depends upon it (such as division). But there is no reason for students who have already grasped subtraction with regrouping to spend any more time on the topic; they should instead be more productively engaged in other topics. Hence teachers need the flexibility to create skill groups when needed, particularly for concepts that are prerequisites for later lessons.

The school's approach to scheduling and deployment of staff must support the formation of short-term skill groups when needed. In addition, the school's organization must allow for skill groups to be formed quickly and changed frequently; flexibility, in other words, is the key.

Implications for Different Levels

I have discussed the above issues separately, as though educators addressed them one at a time. In reality, of course, the various aspects of a school's organizational structure are highly intertwined and tightly related to other aspects of the school, such as curriculum, student assessment, and learning support. Still, there are important differences among schools at different levels.

Elementary Schools

Teacher teams at the elementary-school level may comprise anywhere from two to eight teachers each; more than eight, however, can become unwieldy. These teams may be organized around a single grade level (a "2nd grade team") or as "family" teams of, for example, the 3rd, 4th, and 5th grades. Each arrangement has its advantages and disadvantages. Students in single-grade teams, of course, tend to be closer to one another academically than are those in family teams. On the other hand, these same students must relearn the ropes each year with a different group of teachers, and the teachers must become acquainted with a large new group of students. Academic levels may vary in family teams, but students stay with the same

group of teachers for several years, reducing the startup time required at the beginning of the school year.

Middle Schools

The "middle-school philosophy"—which recognizes that young adolescents learn best when given a fair degree of autonomy, while at the same time "belonging" to a relatively small group of teachers and other students—has become dominant in schools serving the 5th or 6th to 8th grades. Students at this period in their lives experience rapid physical, emotional, and intellectual growth, matched in scope only by the first three years of life; they are experiencing fast and sometimes confusing changes. Middle schools, therefore, must provide both stability and stimulation, respecting the students' age-related concerns.

I have already suggested the major recommendation for middle schools: teachers should work in small teams, composed typically of four teachers, representing the core subjects. Additional subjects should be offered as "exploratory" opportunities for students. In addition, time should be scheduled— *and instruction provided*—in long blocks, permitting teachers the maximum degree of flexibility to meet student needs (and to alter internal arrangements as these needs change). When the school organization allows for the integration of various "support" teachers—Title I, remedial, migrant, gifted, and so on—teachers within each team have the best opportunity to arrange a combination of core and supplementary instruction for each student.

High Schools

Some high schools institute schools-within-a-school (SWAS), often for their 9th grade students.

This structure is designed to mirror (and hence ease the transition from) the middle-school experience. If they can be managed, SWAS are recommended, as they provide students with smaller instructional units and permit them to learn the ropes of the high school—by interacting with a greater number of students and teachers, not to mention abiding by typically more structured rules of conduct—without also having to learn how to find a classroom or juggle the multiple demands of too many different courses.

Scheduling is the main aspect of school organization at the high-school level. Many high schools have by now implemented some form of block scheduling, in which students attend three to four classes on any given day rather than seven to nine. There are two basic patterns for block scheduling: four-by-four and A/B. In four-by-four schedules, students complete four "yearlong" courses each semester in periods of about 90 minutes each day. In the A/B schedule, classes are held on alternate days over the entire year; students may still be carrying six to eight courses, but they attend only half of them on any given day.

In general, block scheduling is advantageous because it provides longer instructional time and more opportunities for engaged learning. When teachers must plan for 90-minute classes, they are likely to employ different approaches than when classes are limited to 40 minutes; they can engage students more deeply in investigations, and will probably vary their instruction more. On the other hand, if teachers don't plan their time effectively, much of it may be wasted; students might devote considerable class time to independent work, for example, that might otherwise be assigned as homework. But in general, block scheduling tends to improve the school climate, with fewer discipline referrals, fewer class changes each day, greater student commitment to the work, and the potential for more engaging instruction.

The two major approaches to high-school block scheduling carry different advantages and disadvantages. Before implementing one or the other, educators are well advised to consult one of the many excellent books that have been written on the subject.

Summary

A school's organizational structures can go a long way toward promoting student learning. At all instructional levels, the school's organizational pattern can materially affect the manner in which students and teachers interact. All of these schoolwide structures should be designed to maximize teacher and student flexibility, encourage in-depth teaching and learning, and integrate as many different resources as possible.

The chart on the following page is intended to help educators examine their own school's approach to school organization and determine whether changes should be made. I have provided a similar chart at the end of each subsequent chapter.

➤ ➤ ➤

	Poor	Basic	Exemplary
RUBRIC FOR SCHOOL ORGANIZATION			
Unit Size	The school has not been divided into subunits; students are assigned to a single teacher in elementary school or to single classes in high school.	Some smaller learning communities have been established as appropriate, but teachers within the subunits do not have the opportunity to engage in joint planning.	The teaming structure allows teachers to work together for the maximum benefit of students; the schedule has been organized to allow for common planning time.
Deployment of Teachers	"Extra" teachers work completely independently of the regular teachers, resulting in fragmented instruction.	Some "extra" teachers are integrated into the regular classroom, but both they and the regular teachers regard their roles as separate and supplemental to student learning in the regular classes.	All teachers in the school work together to maximize the learning of students; "extra" teachers provide their services as part of normal classroom instruction.
Allocation of Space	Space has been allocated for different functions within the school independent of the instructional needs of students and teachers, even when the school building would permit more suitable arrangements.	Only some decisions regarding the use of space are rational and support the school's mission.	Space is allocated to the various functions in ways that maximize the learning of all students. Teachers who work together have easy access to one another, and students can find their way around easily.
Grouping	Permanent instructional groups that divide students according to real or perceived ability are locked into the organizational structure of the school; little or no flexibility to change the groups is possible.	Instructional groups based on ability are not locked into the school's organization, but the school culture does not support flexibility regarding student assignment to different groups.	Teachers are free, within their teams, to move students from group to group as their learning needs change. The school's schedule is organized to permit maximum flexibility for teachers to meet student needs.

6 | Policies and Practices Affecting Students

The policies and practices affecting students are those aspects of a school's operation that organize students' experiences within the institution. For younger students, these policies and practices also structure the parents' relationship with the school. In considering the school's policies and practices affecting students, educators should ask themselves such questions as "What is the school policy with respect to homework, or to 'absences?" "What happens when a student is sent to the principal's office?" "How are students treated in the lunchroom?"

The decisions that a school makes regarding established policies and practices affect students enormously. Teachers' instructional decisions influence students' feelings about (and success with) the curriculum, but the policies and practices in both classrooms and in the entire school provide the context for teacher-student interactions around instruction.

Relationship to the Framework

Decisions regarding policies and practices that affect students should draw from earlier discussions regarding what we want, believe, and know, and should respect the following key concepts.

A Safe and Positive Environment

Both the physical and psychological school environments must be safe for all students. Broken plumbing and falling ceilings, for example, must be fixed in a timely manner. Such problems don't only pose a physical danger; when gone untended, they send a powerful message to students that their well-being is not important. Policies and practices must show respect for students, who should feel safe at school and feel that it is *theirs*. Consistency and predictability are a part of safety; rules and procedures must be fairly and consistently applied, so that they are not regarded as capricious.

A Culture of Hard Work

Students derive enormous satisfaction from tackling difficult tasks and succeeding on their own. If educators want students to experience the pride of success through hard work, they will establish practices that reward hard work rather than natural endowment or luck. In addition, homework and grading policies shouldn't handicap students who don't "get it" on the first attempt; such students should be given a second chance to succeed, and a third.

A Success Orientation

The goal of school policies and practices should be student mastery of the curriculum and development of their potential. There is no room in a school truly committed to student learning for policies that are punitive, turn students away, or undermine their confidence. If some students believe that they are forever relegated to a "low group"—that nothing they do will ever let them become leaders in student government, because they are somehow not regarded as part of the school's "elite"—they will turn their back on the benefits of school. If students regard challenging courses or membership in certain clubs as the province of only a select few, most will harbor no ambitions for such opportunities.

A Culture of Respect and Responsiveness to Clients

In many schools, particularly high schools, students feel that they are the least important people in the building: they are kept waiting by teachers or the principal, they are summoned to the office for mysterious reasons, and they feel that no one ever believes their side of the story. Taken together, the policies and practices in these schools do not produce an environment in which students feel respected as human beings and valued as full participants.

Student Leadership and Decision Making

Opportunities for student leadership can help define the culture of a school. These must not be restricted to an elite—there must be broad opportunities for students to develop leadership skills, such as by helping establish the homework guidelines, serving as lab assistants in science, or lending a hand with younger students.

Decision making relates more to *how* policies and procedures are derived than to what they are. Students of all ages value the opportunity to shape the rules by which they live. When they help create the rules, students are more likely to understand the rationale behind them and will comply with them more willingly. In addition, the inclusion of student voices in the decision-making process provides educators with access to a valuable perspective. Rules and procedures are therefore likely to be stronger if students help create them than they would be if mandated by teachers and administrators alone.

Minimal Competition

Despite knowing the corrosive effects of competition, many educators continue, largely because of tradition, to create policies and practices that institutionalize competitiveness into the fabric of the school. Students should only compete against themselves in the classroom (e.g., by trying to "top" a previous essay).

A Culture for Learning

Learning is an active process, in which students must be engaged as genuine participants. And student learning is not limited to the curriculum: students learn from homework and discipline policies as well. Consequently, aspects of a school's policies that have an effect on student learning should be designed with *active* learning in mind: for example, if educators want students to assume responsibility for their behavior, discipline policies should reflect a view of students as active decision makers.

A school's culture for learning is the implicit sense among students regarding what is valued in the school, and whether it is important to be a successful learner. In this context, I use the term "culture" in the anthropological sense, meaning the norms and values that prevail in a school setting. What is valued? What traits are honored? What are the relative values of athletic skill, academic success, and artistic talent? Many schools, and high schools especially, suffer from a student culture in which it is not "cool" to be smart, work hard, or earn high grades. Educators should bear the following issues in mind when considering their schools' cultures:

➤ **School cultures are slow to change.** Some students, particularly those who have experienced little school success, build their reputa-

tions as class clowns. They project the image that school is dumb, and that only nerds play the game. Even when faculty makes a concerted effort to change this student culture and support a success orientation, the students themselves may be resistant to change. As a result, high-school teachers, particularly in required courses, may inherit students who have had a long history of failure and who are not prepared to risk their self-esteem and reputation with friends for the elusive goal of school success. A shift in school culture will take time.

➤ **Different spheres of student excellence merit recognition.** Most high schools proudly display their athletic trophies, and student athletes are publicly recognized through school assemblies and the student newspaper. Likewise, students with leads in the school play may be acknowledged. But what about a gifted poet? Or the manager of the props for the school play? Or the author of an elegant solution to a mathematics problem? There are many areas of excellent student performance, and a school culture that recognizes only its celebrities can undermine the confidence of students whose talents lie else where.

➤ **A school culture that supports student learning should be promoted both within each classroom and in the school as a whole.** This culture should be promoted in classrooms—where student creativity and commitment should be recognized on a daily basis—as well as throughout the school (e.g., through displays of student work, honor rolls, recognition assemblies, or weekly lunches with the principal).

Categories of Policies and Practices

Schools have multiple policies and practices that affect students. Some of these have been deliberately set in place, and others have evolved with time. Educators are well advised to re-examine the accepted ways of doing things at their schools. These practices will be familiar to both students and faculty, and if they contribute to a school's focus on learning, they should be retained. Practices that do not support student learning should be revised to ensure that they *do,* difficult though it may be to disrupt the status quo.

The major policies and practices affecting students are described below.

Attendance Policies

Most schools establish their attendance policies on the assumption that the students can't learn unless they are in school. The goal of such policies is to ensure that students attend school as much as possible. Of course, no school wants to encourage students who are sick to attend school, lest they infect others. Unfortunately, students will occasionally be sick without even knowing it, thereby infecting other students before being sent home. (Many elementary teachers have had the experience of chicken pox working its way through their class for most of an entire school year.)

In general, attendance policies should do the following:

➤ **Maximize time in school.** Attendance and tardiness policies should be grounded in the expectation that school is not optional and that attendance is important. However, staff members must allow for illness and recognize mitigating circumstances. Schools should therefore probably not set an absolute limit to absences, but might require statements from parents or doctors explaining why the child has missed school.

➤ **Be flexible.** Attendance and tardiness policies must allow for individual circumstances and for situations outside of a student's control, such as the need to care for younger siblings.

➤ **Offer opportunities for teaching.** Students of all ages can benefit from learning how to improve attendance and punctuality. In most cases, this opportunity for teaching can be achieved in the classroom setting: students can share strategies for preparing their school materials in advance of when they must walk out the door, or for ensuring that they make the bus. However, some students—particularly older students who face challenges at home—may need individual coaching. A counselor or trusted teacher can be of real assistance in these cases.

Discipline Policies

Discipline policies are the rules regarding student conduct, both within classrooms and in the school as a whole. These include rules about running in the halls, disrespectful language, willful disregard of teacher requests, and, for older students, public displays of affection. Discipline policies might also include student conduct on the bus and playground, or in the cafeteria.

In a sincere attempt to enhance the quality of their school environment, educators in some schools have instituted harsh zero-tolerance policies for students. In some cases, such as weapons possession, a zero-tolerance approach is certainly justified. However, it is important that educators not confuse being tough with being businesslike.

Educators must appreciate the relationship between instruction and student conduct. When students are engaged in meaningful work and experience learning success, they are not much inclined to disrupt a class. But if students are bored, or if they believe that they are about to be embarrassed or humiliated, they may actually prefer being sent to the office to staying in class. A solution, then, for some student infractions may be to make learning experiences more engaging, so that students can be challenged as well as successful.

Successful standards of conduct will reflect certain characteristics:

➤ **Respectful and appropriate.** Discipline policies should reflect a school's belief that everyone in the school community—both adults and students—must be treated with respect (e.g., no bullying or impolite language). Consequences for student infractions should fit the situation, and should not be punitive; students should not be suspended for trivial infractions.

➤ **Public.** Standards of student conduct should be well publicized and known to everyone: students, teachers, and parents. They need to be, and to be *perceived* to be, reasonable and transparent; any appearance of arbitrariness will undermine their credibility.

➤ **Consistent.** Standards of student conduct should be consistent across a school, rather than dependent on the whim of each teacher. Individual teachers may have their own expectations, of course, but the same general rules should apply across an entire school.

Homework Policies

Teachers assign homework to students mainly to extend learning time. Students are in school for six hours or so each day; if they complete assignments at home, they can be actively engaged in learning for considerably longer than that.

A school's approach to homework depends on the age of the students. Although it is unreasonable to expect young children to spend long hours doing assignments, a well-conceived homework policy helps students assume more responsibility for their own learning and allows students to continue learning beyond the school day.

As educators determine their school's approach to homework, the following guidelines may be helpful:

➤ **Homework is important.** If assigned, homework must be completed; it should not be optional, but rather integral to the instructional program. A school's homework policy should convey the importance the school attaches to homework and emphasize student commitment and responsibility for completing it.

➤ **Students must be able to complete assignments independently.** As a general rule, students should be able to complete assignments without adult assistance at home. The reason for this is simple equity. Some parents are able to substantially assist their children by virtue of their own education: they can explain how to factor polynomials, for example, or provide feedback on writing. But because other parents are not able to offer this type of help, only *some* students will have the benefit of what amounts to a private tutor at home. It is essential that success in school not depend on the availability of parental assistance.

➤ **Assignments should be appropriate to completion at home.** Some assignments are inappropriate for homework—such as those that represent new learning or learning that requires frequent explanations or intervention by a teacher. More suitable homework assignments are those that ask students to practice previously learned skills, write essays, or memorize vocabulary. Practice increases fluency and facility, and repetition can enhance student mastery of a concept.

➤ **Links between home and school should be pursued.** Some assignments can integrate the home into the learning experience. After studying the Great Depression, for example, 11th grade history students might be asked to interview older relatives and neighbors regarding their experiences during the Depression and its aftermath. Or 3rd graders, after having learned to make bar graphs, can collect data regarding the different types of furniture in their homes and display the information in a bar chart; the next day, the classroom walls will be covered with charts of chairs, tables, beds, and televisions from which patterns may be observed and hypotheses generated.

➤ **Educators should help students deal with emergencies.** When unforeseen events occur, students should not be unduly penalized. Some students, however, exhibit a pattern of suspicious "emergencies"—dogs, after all, can eat only so much paper. Teachers may need to help such students to develop a "plan B" that they can implement when emergencies arise.

➤ **Teachers should distinguish between completion and effort.** Students sometimes get stuck in the course of doing their homework

because they do not understand something critical. This may be due to poor instruction, lack of clarity about the assignment, or day dreaming on the part of the student during an explanation. But the result is that the home work is not complete. A reasonable and respectful policy will take these factors into account. In addition, teachers should ask students to document what they did before abandoning their homework: what approaches they tried, for example, or the names of students they phoned for help. Such a policy sends the message that perseverance and resourcefulness are important, so students should not give up at the first sign of trouble.

➤ **Teachers should coordinate major assignments.** Students are quick to notice when major assignments from two different courses are due on the same day, and they are not completely open to their teachers' suggestions that a little advance planning would mitigate the conflict. If a school wants students to give energy to the work they do outside of school, it makes sense for teachers in different departments to share their schedules for major assignments with one another. Students should certainly be expected to complete small daily assignments in many subjects, but major assignments should be coordinated.

➤ **Teachers should help parents help their children.** A school's staff should support a richer intellectual environment at home for students, independent of homework, by encouraging parental involvement. Educators should enlighten parents who don't recognize the educational value of regularly reading aloud to younger children, or of asking them to set the table or sort the laundry. Older children can be asked to read bus schedules or road maps on car trips, or to determine which brand of soap is the best bargain at the supermarket—skills that require higher-order thinking. And children of all ages benefit from conversation or keeping a journal. Educators should help parents to appreciate the value of these activities, so that they will encourage their children to take part in them.

Grading Policies

Of all the policies and practices affecting students, the school's approach to grading has the greatest potential to affect students' futures, both within the school and beyond it. Furthermore, a school's grading policy will often have a lot of "baggage" associated with it, as it is an aspect of school life about which everyone—teachers, students, and parents—feels strongly.

Almost no one believes that conventional approaches to grading are beneficial. There is no consensus as to what grades mean; some teachers appear to believe that their grade distributions reflect their own teaching abilities or the complexity of the content more than they do student achievement; others maintain that their harsh grading policy reflects their own high standards. Teachers also tend to disagree on the quality of student work: given the same student essay, some teachers would award it an *A* while others would give it a *C*. Teachers, that is, tend to apply their own standards of quality to student work that are rarely communicated to either students or other teachers. Furthermore, many citizens, educators, and admissions directors in institutions of higher education think that the distribution of grades should follow the bell curve, believing that too many high grades is evidence of grade inflation.

Any discussion of grading policies must begin with their purposes, which include the following:

➤ **Motivating students.** Educators can use grades to motivate students to work hard, study, and learn the content of a course, especially in high school.

➤ **Communicating with students.** Grades can help let students know what learning is important, as well as how well they are doing, in general.

➤ **Communicating with parents.** Grades can help let parents know how well their children are progressing in school. Most parents are not interested in the details of their children's progress; they are primarily looking for reassurance that their children are "on track."

➤ **Communicating with other teachers.** In some schools, teachers use grades to let one another know how well students are performing. When students move from one school to another—from middle school to high school, for example—grades can be used to communicate between the two faculties.

➤ **Communicating with the outside world.** Admissions directors at colleges, universities, and technical schools, as well as company personnel directors, look to school transcripts for clues about students. Educational institutions want to know whether students are sufficiently prepared for the rigors of higher education, whereas employers tend to care about factors such as punctuality, interpersonal skills, and initiative.

The following recommendations are based on the assumptions threaded throughout this book. Grading is a complex topic on which it is difficult to achieve consensus. The recommendations I offer here will, I hope, serve as a basis for structured conversation on the subject.

Reflective of Student Learning in the Curriculum

A grade for English on a report card should reflect how well the student has *mastered the content* of the English course; if teachers want to comment on participation, effort, or behavior in class, they may do so on the report card, but not as part of a grade. Students' effort, homework, behavior, and attendance are all important aspects of their work in school, and should be part of any comprehensive report to parents. However, when these are incorporated into the grading system, the grades become muddled and therefore meaningless.

In addition, an individual student's grades should be allocated independently of any other student. If all students master the curriculum at a high level, they should all receive *A*s or *B*s.

Consistency Within a School

An *A* from Ms. Jones should mean the same as an *A* from Mr. Smith; grades should not reflect each teacher's idiosyncratic notions of what constitutes quality. Consistency within a school (or even a district), combined with the need for grades to reflect student learning in the curriculum, suggests that teachers have decided together what the curriculum is and how to assess it. It implies, in other words, the use of consistent assessments at the end of courses or semesters. (This issue is further addressed in Chapter 10: Assessment.)

Multiple Measures of Student Learning

Within the context of a consistent approach to curriculum and assessment, individual teachers need to consider many different indicators of student mastery of the curriculum when assigning grades. An end-of-course exam for Algebra I that is used consistently throughout the mathematics department may be a valuable benchmark of student work, but it should not be the only factor used to determine student grades in the course; teachers should consider quizzes, projects, and oral presentations as well. Learning, and the demonstration of that learning, is what's important—not student performance on a single high-stakes test.

Grade Inflation

Many observers have noted that grades "just aren't what they used to be." Commentators have bemoaned the fact that, even in the most selective schools and colleges, it is common for a majority of students to receive *A*s or *B*s, thus rendering the grades effectively meaningless. Some argue that the professors who hand out such grades are under pressure from students to "doctor the books" and boost their chances at graduate school admission or good jobs. These complaints are worthy of serious attention when

➤ Grades reflect only the idiosyncratic judgments of individual teachers,

➤ Students have no way to improve their performance,

➤ Grades are handed out as rewards for compliance in class, or

➤ Grades have little connection to student performance.

If, however, grades actually reflect student understanding of the curriculum, then large numbers of high grades should be applauded rather than criticized, as this means simply that many students are mastering important concepts.

Complaints about grade inflation make sense only in the context of general confusion about the fundamental meaning of grades. If more students are earning higher grades, and if high grades represent high levels of achievement, then everyone should be cheering. On the other hand, if more and more students are getting *A*'s but nobody knows what the grades actually mean, then the concerned voices have an important message.

Summary

The nature of students' experience in school is influenced not only by the quality of instruction, but also by the school's policies and practices. Students of all ages approach school with a positive spirit, and they expect to find success and fulfillment there, so the policies and practices affecting them must be clear, fair, and likely to contribute to student learning. Such policies can be firm, but they should also be just, and should respect student interests and motivations. Policies and practices affecting students are powerful levers that help set the tone and direct behavior in a school. The adults involved must ensure that the policies they put in place reinforce their goals for students, reflect their beliefs about students and their learning, and are supported by research findings.

➤   ➤   ➤

	Poor	Basic	Exemplary
RUBRIC FOR POLICIES AND PRACTICES AFFECTING STUDENTS			
A Culture for Learning	The school has no culture for learning, or a negative culture. Students appear satisfied to "just get by."	Some of the school's practices reinforce the culture for learning; students have partially internalized this culture and some of them make a commitment to excellence.	School practices reinforce the culture for learning; students have internalized this culture and make a serious commitment to excellence.
Attendance Policies	Attendance and tardiness policies are rigid and punitive; no attention is paid to student learning or flexibility for individual situations. Students have had no opportunity to contribute to the development of the policies.	Attendance and tardiness policies are focused on maximizing attendance, but are only partially flexible for individual situations. Students have had some opportunity to contribute to the development of the policies.	Attendance and tardiness policies are focused on maximizing attendance and student learning, and are flexible and responsive to individual situations. Students have contributed to the development of the policies.
Discipline Policies	Standards of student conduct are arbitrary, and consequences for student infractions are punitive and harsh. Discipline policies are not well publicized and students have had no opportunity to contribute to their development.	Standards of student conduct and the consequences for student infractions are fairly reasonable. Discipline policies are publicly known and students have had some opportunity to contribute to their development.	Standards of student conduct are based on mutual respect, and consequences for student infractions are reasonable. Discipline policies are publicly known and students have contributed to their development.
Homework Policies	Homework policies and practices are rigid and not designed to promote student learning. Consequences of incomplete homework are punitive. Students have had no opportunity to contribute to the development of the policies.	Homework policies and practices are moderately flexible and attempt to promote student learning. Consequences for incomplete homework are fairly reasonable. Students have had some opportunity to contribute to the development of the policies.	Homework policies and practices are flexible and designed to promote student learning. Consequences for incomplete homework are firm but respectful. Students have contributed to the development of the policies.
Grading Policies	Student grades are awarded according to the bell curve; factors other than mastery of the curriculum, such as cooperation, are used to inflate poor grades; or grades are awarded to students based on the teachers' individual preferences and favoritism towards students.	Teachers decide grades according to a combination of factors that are poorly articulated and not well understood by students and parents. Grades reflect not only mastery of the curriculum, but also effort, amount of progress, and level of participation and cooperation.	Student grades reflect mastery of the curriculum, and do not reflect the standing of students relative to other students. Factors such as effort, amount of progress, and level of participation and cooperation are addressed separately on report cards.

7

Policies and Practices Affecting Staff

Policies and practices affecting staff define the working environment for adults within a school. These policies and practices encompass all established decision-making procedures, expectations of staff performance and responsibilities, and staff appraisals and professional development opportunities.

As with the policies and practices affecting students, those affecting staff tend to reflect the values of the people who have created them. Schools are, among many other things, cultural institutions: they have norms and values in place that affect how people are treated and how they treat one another. There are many other rules, both formal and informal. Above all, schools are *professional* organizations, in which individuals motivated by a shared vision come together for a specific and meaningful purpose.

Relationship to the Framework

As with other aspects of a school's culture, policies and practices affecting staff must reflect the aspirations and values embodied within the framework for school improvement. Explicit recognition of these connections can help educators maintain consistent approaches to policymaking.

Focus on Student Learning

All of a school's organizational structures affecting staff must be designed with an unwavering focus on student learning. It is all too easy to confuse means with ends and focus on procedures rather than results. Procedures for teacher evaluation, instructional planning, and professional development should all be organized around their demonstrated impact on student learning.

A Safe and Positive Environment for Learning

Just as a school's environment must be safe and positive for students, so must it be for adults. Fear shuts people down: if teachers are to try new approaches in their classrooms, they must feel safe from recrimination if their efforts don't go smoothly at first. The school culture must be one of open exploration, or else teachers and other staff will not dare to try new things. Furthermore, a culture of professional inquiry involves learning of new approaches; teachers, no less than their students, learn best when they play an active role. Therefore, policies and practices governing professional development and evaluation must actively engage teachers in the process.

A Culture of Respect

Adults as well as students must be treated with respect. There is no place in a school for teachers who undermine the efforts of their colleagues or score points at their expense. Instead they should exult in one another's successes and support their coworker's endeavors: teachers who attain certification by the National Board for Professional Teaching Standards should find their success celebrated by their colleagues, rather than having to conceal the honor for fear of censure. Educators should not feel as though they're competing with one another for the principal's approval or for recognition by the central office. In addition, teachers in a respectful environment play an active role in the formulation

of policies and practices that affect them, and assume responsibility for the results.

All Work Has Value and Dignity

It is not only teachers and administrators who create a school culture for students; the custodial, cafeteria, and office staffs contribute greatly as well. The secretary's smile, the lunch lady's encouraging comment, and the custodian's explanation of how something works can create a positive environment that may not be evident in some student's interactions with teachers and administrators. Noninstructional staff members, in other words, should be considered full members of the school team.

Categories of Policies and Practices Affecting Staff

Expectations of Employment

Every school has expectations regarding its staff, covering such issues as punctuality, attendance at required faculty meetings and workshops, completion of required paperwork (such as attendance and grade reports or supply orders), and participation in school functions (for example, back-to-school night or the science fair). Some of these expectations are articulated in the school personnel manual; others are simply understood. It is helpful to all concerned, however, if all expectations are stated explicitly.

School or district expectations set the ground rules for all staff members. They convey what is expected of everyone and therefore what teachers can expect of everyone else. For example, teachers can expect their colleagues to at least turn up for work and hand in their grade reports. There is nothing particularly inspirational about such expectations, but they should be clear and explicitly communicated.

Expectations should also reflect what is in the best interest of students; they are not intended merely for the convenience of the staff. If teachers are expected to participate in parent conferences, it should be because such participation is important for student learning. Similarly, if teachers are expected to make curriculum decisions with their instructional teams, it should be to help yield a coherent curriculum to the benefit of students.

Decision-Making and Budgeting Systems

Schools must make hundreds of decisions a year related to all aspects of their operations, and because many choices entail costs, decision-making systems are in effect budgeting systems as well. School approaches to decision making vary greatly: some schools allow decisions to be made only at the very top, whereas others are much more democratic; some have elaborate networks of teams or site councils while others leave decisions to a small group of people (typically administrators and department chairs or team leaders). Some teachers want to be involved in the details of every decision, while others would prefer to leave decision making to colleagues ("Those are administrative matters—let the administrators do them").

A school's budgeting and decision-making systems should be clear to everyone, and anyone who wants to participate should have the opportunity to do so. If purchases are deferred, the reasons behind the deferral should be clear and should make sense to everyone, and all staff members should adhere to the new timetable. People don't mind waiting in line if they know they are in line;

what they can't tolerate is for others—personal friends of the principal, for instance—to jump the queue for a pet project.

Instructional Planning

Many noneducators are astonished to learn how little communication occurs among educators within a school. In many schools, teachers work almost in complete isolation: they prepare for their own classes on their own, develop their own tests, and submit grades when they are due. Such teachers work almost as independent contractors: they are hired to do a job and they do it, but not as members of a team. This isolation is detrimental to a school committed to successful learning by all students, as the teachers cannot be aware of approaches and strategies that others have found successful, and might even be working at cross purposes without even knowing it.

Joint instructional planning that is systematic, disciplined, and skilled is one of the most powerful tools a school can use to meet its goals for students. Of course, successful team planning does not happen by accident; it must first be pre-arranged and accorded a high priority. When well organized, the benefits of team planning—both to the students' education and to teacher commitment and morale—are enormous, and have been well documented in the business world as well as in the world of education. Good teamwork creates an environment of mutual support and common purpose that is virtually impossible for individuals to create and sustain on their own. When teams are working well together, the whole is a great deal more than the sum of the parts.

A school's arrangement into teams or houses, together with an expectation that teachers will engage in joint planning, affects the type and extent of teacher collaboration. The school schedule must permit teachers to plan instruction and make decisions collaboratively; schools typically accomplish this by setting aside common planning time for teachers.

Professional Development

Anyone who has ever worked as a teacher can attest to the complexity of the role. Students are individual human beings, all with their own backgrounds, hopes, interests, and aptitudes. Marshalling student energy in the service of learning and meeting school goals requires teachers to be intelligent, flexible, creative, and dynamic. Because of demographic shifts, professional development offerings must include opportunities for teachers to learn more about the populations they serve and recommendations for working with students and communities of different backgrounds.

Educators would have to be arrogant to believe that their study of teaching is complete. To argue that a school should take professional development seriously is not to suggest that the teaching is poor and needs "fixing"; instead, it reflects the difficulty and complexity of the job. Educators can always learn more about the subjects they teach and how best to help students understand them.

One important source of professional insight is located right within the school's walls: the expertise of staff. Along with research studies and professional reports, the work of colleagues can provide valuable information for educators. A school's professional development plan, therefore, should include both internal and external sources of new ideas. A culture of professional inquiry that presumes high-level teaching skills and is embedded

in an ethos of sharing will energize teachers to learn new techniques.

Peer observations are one practical manifestation of such a culture. Observations of teaching are widely used, of course, in the context of teacher evaluation, but they can also be used as part of a professional development program. In some schools, teachers are taught how to offer nonjudgmental feedback prior to observing their colleagues at work. But the presumption of these types of practices is that the beneficiary of all such observations is the person being observed, whether the observer is an evaluator or a peer. However, observations can be used as the cornerstone of an entirely different approach in which the beneficiary of the observation is the observer. Thus, if a teacher is searching for new techniques in some aspect of teaching—for example, in leading class discussions—a valuable component of a professional development plan might be to observe colleagues using that skill in the classroom. This observation can be followed by a discussion about how and why the teacher used certain methods.

A school's approach to mentoring new teachers, particularly those new to the profession, provides yet another opportunity for professional growth. To argue for the importance of mentoring is not to suggest that preparation programs are deficient, but to emphasize the complexity of teaching and recognize that educators can learn some aspects of teaching only once they've become teachers of record. As with driving a car, some skills simply cannot be simulated, and virtually all new teachers benefit from structured support as they acquire those skills. I must emphasize that "structured support" should consist of far more than just a buddy system: emotional support, though critical, is not sufficient for learning to teach. A structured induction program focused on instructional skill is essential. And when teachers receive such support they are much more likely to remain in the profession; the attrition rates for teachers with mentors is far lower than it is for those without such a program: a study of 125 new teacher support programs in California reported a retention rate for first- and second-year teachers of 93 percent (WestEd, 2001).

Of course, new teachers aren't the only ones who benefit from mentoring; the mentors do as well. Experienced teachers who serve as mentors (particularly in a structured program) routinely report that the experience makes them better teachers, encouraging them to reflect on their own teaching and providing new insights into their work. The professional conversations that accompany a good mentoring program can help establish or reinforce a culture of inquiry among the professional staff in a school.

Teacher Evaluation

A school's approach to teacher evaluation sets the tone for much of its professional culture. Typically, teacher evaluations are a function of district policy, and a result of negotiated agreements between the school and district. Still, teacher evaluation happens at school, and is greatly influenced by the personalities of and relationships among school staff. I offer here a brief summary of the recommendations for teacher evaluation provided in my book *Teacher Evaluation to Enhance Professional Practice* (2000), cowritten with Thomas McGreal.

There are two fundamental purposes for teacher evaluation: quality assurance and profes-

sional learning. Teacher evaluation systems are the only systems a school or district has to ensure that every student is taught by a competent professional; the system *must* be able to make that guarantee. But because the vast majority of teachers are competent—and most are excellent—the evaluation system should help improve as well as assess teacher practice.

In many school districts, the requirements and procedures are different for experienced teachers than they are for novice teachers. This is because the district needs to learn different things from different types of teachers: in the case of probationary teachers, for example, the district needs to ensure that it offers continuing contracts only to teachers it's willing to commit to for the long term. Differentiated systems recognize that novice and experienced teachers also have different needs: whereas teachers who are just beginning their careers need a lot of support and guidance, their more experienced colleagues can to a large degree monitor and assess themselves.

Carefully designed evaluation systems can offer teachers valuable opportunities to reflect on their practice and enhance their skills. Teachers may be asked to explain their instructional goals for students, demonstrate their approaches to student assessment, or describe an assignment using samples of student work. These activities offer evidence of teachers' skills while also allowing them to engage in self-assessment and reflection, which can lead to improved practice.

A school's system of teacher evaluation, then, is an important aspect of its professional culture, and must convey both respect for teachers and high expectations for performance. Such a system should also establish a common language for describing good teaching while encouraging teachers to be flexible when trying to achieve their goals with students.

Support Staff

Teachers and administrators are arguably the staff members most critical to student learning; after all, they are the ones who work with students and engage them in the classroom. According to this perspective, anything important that happens with students is due the work of the professional staff.

This is a shortsighted and limited view. Members of the support staff also play an essential role in students' school experiences, and should be regarded as full partners in the effort. When students (and certainly their parents) enter the school's office, a secretary greets them; school-bus drivers, cafeteria workers, and playground aides also set the cultural tone for their areas of work, and custodians and maintenance workers help keep the school running while serving as additional adult role models for students. The entire staff, not only the teachers and administrators, creates the culture of a school.

Because of their critical role in establishing the school's culture and implementing its policies, support staff members should also help revise those policies. Members of the office staff will have insights about how to make a new attendance policy work, for example, and thus should contribute to its development.

The inclusion of support staff in the life of the school extends beyond helping to develop policies and practices. Because support-staff members make important contributions to the life of the school, they should be invited to full-staff meetings and parties; they should not, in other words, be made to feel like second-class citizens. Faculty-only meetings for working on instructional matters have their place, of course, but the school is more than only the instructional program.

Summary

Policies and practices affecting staff must be subject to the same screening process as everything else in the school: they must support student learning and a culture of professional inquiry, treat all individuals with respect, include all staff members in matters that affect them, and adhere to what is known from the research literature about professionalism and professional growth.

➤ ➤ ➤

	Poor	Basic	Exemplary
Expectations for Employment	Employment expectations are arbitrary, do not promote student learning, have been developed without teacher involvement, or are not clearly communicated,.	Expectations for employment are reasonable, partially help promote some student learning, were developed with some involvement by teachers and have been clearly communicated.	Expectations for employment are focused on the advancement of student learning, have been developed with full involvement by teachers, and are clearly communicated to all staff.
Decision-Making and Budgeting Systems	Decision-making and budgeting systems are secretive and involve only a few teachers in the processes. There is no screening process to ensure that the decisions made will support student learning.	Decision-making and budgeting systems are moderately clear to everyone, and permit some teachers to be involved in the processes. The processes yield decisions that may support student learning.	Decision-making and budgeting systems are transparent to everyone, and permit all teachers to be involved in the processes. The processes yield decisions that unambiguously support student learning.
Joint Instructional Planning	Teachers work in complete isolation from their colleagues; attempts at joint planning are dysfunctional and regarded as a waste of time.	The school staff attempts to implement systems of joint instructional planning, which are moderately successful but are undermined by a lack of sufficient resources, time, or skills.	Teachers engage in highly productive joint instructional planning that results in higher levels of student learning. Teachers value the time they spend with colleagues, and find that it strengthens their practice.
Professional Development	Professional development decisions are made at the top, and teachers are afforded little opportunity to determine what avenues to pursue. The professional atmosphere in the school is closed and isolated.	Teachers have some input into professional development offerings, although they are primarily designed by others. Teachers have limited opportunities to work with colleagues. The culture of professional inquiry is fairly positive.	Teachers design the professional development offerings in the school, in order to improve student learning and meet the school's goals. The culture of professional inquiry is open, and provides teachers with multiple opportunities to collaborate on their work.
Teacher Evaluation	The system for teacher evaluation is hierarchical and punitive; teachers are not informed of the evaluative criteria, evaluators lack the skills to observe performances fairly and accurately or provide feedback, and neither teachers nor evaluators have confidence in the system.	The system for teacher evaluation is fair but does not offer opportunities for teachers to enhance their practice. Evaluative criteria are fairly clear to everyone, and evaluators have had some exposure to the skills of consistent observation and providing feedback.	The system for teacher evaluation is highly rewarding for both teachers and evaluators, emphasizing professional learning as well as quality assurance. Evaluative criteria are clear and acceptable to everyone, and evaluators are able to make consistent judgments of performance and provide valuable feedback.
Support Staff	The support staff is excluded from decision-making procedures and regarded by teachers and students alike as "second-class citizens."	The support staff is partially incorporated into the life of the school, and permitted to make minor contributions to the development of policies and procedures.	The support staff is fully incorporated into the life of the school and makes material contributions to the development of policies and procedures.

8

Linkages Beyond the School

Schools engage with their communities in both a physical and a functional sense: as *buildings,* their spaces can be used for multiple purposes; as *institutions,* they share certain goals with other agencies and individuals in the community. When mutually supportive, the relationship between schools and communities can lead to shared programs for the benefit of all. Students and teachers can link up with individuals and institutions beyond the school in a variety of ways, ranging from simple communication with parents and others in the community to jointly run services and mentoring opportunities.

Relationship to the Framework

The linkages that a school staff forges with individuals and institutions beyond its walls should reflect the school's goals and beliefs about students and their learning.

High-Level Learning and Success for All Students

The relationships between a school and its external partners (such as parents, community agencies, other educational institutions, or businesses) should focus primarily on advancing student learning. When school staff members link to outside individuals and agencies, they are constantly aware of the effect those connections have on student learning—whether they are communicating with parents, receiving or passing along information to other schools, or arranging student internships with local businesses.

The School as a Learning Community for Students, Faculty, and the Larger Community

Educators who want their school to be seen as a center of learning for the larger community should carefully consider the recommendations in this chapter. Linking to the world outside of school can take a number of forms, usually including an adult-education program.

Responsiveness to Clients

When educators communicate with university faculty and admission directors or with business leaders, they should never forget that these individuals are clients of the school just as much as parents and students are. Because universities and employers will inherit students, they care that the schools have done their jobs well. Therefore, educators must attend to the very real interests of others in the community in the successful education of young people. Although educators are tempted at times to regard parents, business leaders, and others as distractions from their "real" work (i.e., teaching students), it is important to recognize them as the clients they are.

Communication

Communication is essential when schools forge links with the broader community, and can include sharing information about individual students, the school's program, and services to and from the community.

Communication with Families and Caregivers

Much of the communication with families and other caregivers is the responsibility of individual teachers, and can be accomplished using such means as newsletters, phone calls, and notes. Teachers should inform parents both about the instructional program and about the progress of individual students. Given the electronic technology now available, many teachers find that they can provide access to students and their parents regarding such things as grading policies, homework assignments, and additional resources for students and parents. As this technology becomes more widely available, educators will take increasing advantage of it.

Of course, many schools have institutional procedures in place as well, including report cards, back-to-school nights, evenings devoted to specific curricular areas (such as "math nights" or poetry readings), seasonal concerts, student-led conferences, and displays of student work. As for information about students, individual teachers' efforts may be supplemented by schoolwide procedures such as midterm "warning notices" that alert parents to individual students' difficulties. Of course, the communication should be mutual; teachers must hear from families when they have concerns or information to share—they are truly partners in the educational effort.

Many schools and districts take their communication responsibilities seriously. For example, many schools create materials that describe what the school or district expects students to learn in each curricular area, and share the rubrics used to assess student work. These materials provide parents with a summary of what their children will be learning at different stages of their education. Some schools post information about the school and about individual courses on a Web site.

Communication with Other Educators

Schools are not islands; they exist within a web of educational institutions that all serve the same students. The students' best interests are served if these institutions have methods in place for communicating with one another. Educators at different levels of schooling must devise strategies for sharing information about individual students. Progress reports are one such strategy, and for many students they will be sufficient. But for students who have unique ways of learning, difficulty in certain types of settings, or unfamiliar backgrounds and cultures, additional strategies may be required.

Educators should also share information about their respective instructional programs with colleagues at other schools. In many districts, there is little awareness among different levels of schooling from one school to another; for example, a "neat" approach to teaching writing at a middle school may be completely unknown to the English teachers at the high school that the students will attend.

If students are to be successful in their postsecondary studies, their professors must understand the instructional program at their old schools as well as how successful the students were in the program. This is particularly important if the program in question is especially innovative or easily misunderstood.

Communication with the Business Community

The business community cares deeply about the quality of local public schools—after all, these schools produce the vast majority of their future employees. In general, the more a business community knows about the schools, the more supportive of them it will be. As with parents, communication with the business community should be mutual. Business leaders may provide schools with important feedback about their programs that can help teachers to emphasize elements, such as teamwork, that are important to employers.

Many schools formalize their communications with the business community—for example, by asking the president of a local company to serve on its site council (thereby contributing to the school's decision-making process). In addition, teachers can invite business leaders to speak with students about their fields, opportunities at their companies for graduates, and training and educational requirements for different professions.

Collaboration with Public and Private Agencies

Partnerships between schools and public or private community agencies can have a powerful effect on student learning. These agencies serve many different populations and offer a variety of services, but the advantages of collaboration are similar for all: increased effectiveness, improved offerings, and a reduced amount of duplication.

Partnerships to Improve the School's Program

Most communities contain plenty of resources—museums and zoos, for example—that can strengthen a school's instructional program. Indeed, many of these resources include programs for students as part of their missions, and some even offer opportunities for students to engage in community service work. These resources include:

➤ **School trips.** Most schools include trips as part of their instructional program. These are frequently memorable to students, and can include excursions to the zoo, the local fire station, a play or musical production, or a factory, among many others. Such excursions must serve to advance student learning, and should be tied to specific content standards. If students are well-prepared and approach the trip with specific questions or goals in mind, their outings will prove instructive. The principal value of any trip lies in the students' opportunities for structured reflection afterwards by sharing observations and exploring questions that may lead to additional study.

➤ **Visitors.** Guests to the school can greatly enhance the instructional program if their visits are tied to a specific purpose. But students must be prepared: they should formulate questions beforehand to learn as much as possible from the visitor. Some visitors—artists-in-residence, for instance—can contribute to the school's program over an extended period of time. These individuals can acquaint students with perspectives to which they would otherwise have little access; students can see how an artist actually works, for example, or learn stories from a master storyteller. Many visitors can be arranged at no cost to the school: police and fire officials, parents of students, and retired members of the community will frequently come for free. Other visitors, such as artists, poets, or musicians, will usually require compensation; many earn their livings visiting schools. Affluent school districts will often fund such activities; less wealthy communities might approach local businesses for support. In some areas, government grants are specifically earmarked for cultural programs, including visitors.

➤ **Community-service opportunities.** Many schools have discovered the power of community-service programs to help students understand the lives of others and learn the rewards of sharing and service. Students who engage in these activities will also learn how community agencies operate and to appreciate the role such organizations play in the life of a community. They see people doing real jobs, serving others; for many students these adults serve as important role models as they formulate their own future plans.

Partnerships with Community Agencies

All communities finance agencies other than public schools that are devoted to the well-being of their citizens. Many of these agencies would be stronger, and would serve the public better, if they operated more closely with local schools.

➤ **Community education.** In many communities, the adult-education program operates in public schools at night. Such arrangements make perfect sense, as they allow facilities to be used when they otherwise wouldn't be. In these cases, schools must make arrangements regarding custodial services, use of supplies, and the like. The same facilities can also be used during the summer months, when regular students are absent; members of the community who are able to attend during the day can benefit enormously from this type of extended program.

➤ **Health services.** Most communities already have public health clinics for well-baby visits, immunizations, and public health communication. School health programs also address community concerns: for example, many school nurses verify that the students have had certain immunizations before enrolling them in school. In schools with room to spare, it might be possible to locate community health programs within the school.

➤ **Libraries.** Public libraries can be merged with school libraries to provide a public library close to the homes of many citizens. Such a setup allows the school library to stay open long past school hours, and can save the community money by avoiding the duplication of books and periodicals and by employing a single staff to serve both the school and the public. When students work in the library alongside members of the community, they come to see the library as a place of lifelong learning by adults, rather than of student drudgery. The library may even institute programs specifically to serve the students, such as an after-school children's program.

Collaboration with the Business Community

The importance of ongoing communication with the business community has been described above, but beyond communication is the possibility of larger collaboration.

Learning Opportunities for Students

There is nothing like "real" work to help students put their schooling in perspective and understand the relevance of their schoolwork. In-depth participation in a local business—as a helper in a television studio, a gofer in a law firm, or a receptionist in a doctor's office—can introduce students to entire careers of which they had little awareness beforehand. It is essential, however, that students be prepared for such experiences. They should know how to dress and how to carry themselves appropriately, and some may need to be told that they should speak formal English in the workplace. Meaningful engagement in a business environment may open doors on which the students had not even thought to knock.

Many business owners need convincing that it is in their interest to welcome students into their establishments. Some employers might consider the presence of a student for even a few hours a week to be too much of a distraction; they may think that students require such high levels of supervision that they cannot afford to have them around. These fears should be dispelled if possible. Business leaders must be convinced that making opportunities available to students is in their own long-term interest as well as in the best interest of students: by initiating students to the world of adult work and showing them alternatives to careers in fast food, employers introduce students to the many possibilities for work (and education) that they might want to pursue.

Learning and Working Opportunities for Teachers

Many enlightened business establishments—particularly those with an emphasis on science, such as pharmaceutical companies—have discovered the mutual benefits of hiring teachers for the summer. For teachers, the benefits are obvious: they get to see close-up how scientific knowledge is used day-to-day in the business world, and to witness firsthand how quickly companies absorb such knowledge.

There are benefits to the businesses, no less than for the educators. Teachers bring an intellectual curiosity with them, which they apply to any situation at hand. Teachers are adept at problem solving (they do it all day every day at school!). A teacher's skills and perspectives, while somewhat different than those of a career chemist, for example, will likely shed new light on situations within a company, yielding a more productive approach than would have been the case without their participation.

Collaboration with Universities

Universities are natural partners for schools. Colleges of education, in particular, deal with the same issues as practicing educators, albeit from a typically more theoretical standpoint. The range of potential partnerships is virtually endless, and can include the following aims.

Meeting the Needs of Individual Students

High school programs will occasionally be unable to meet a student's needs. In these cases, schools should seek assistance from local universities. For example, if only three students are ready for calculus, the best way for them to get the course may be to enroll in calculus at the local university. Such arrangements are not perfect, of course: transportation must be arranged, and the schedules of the two schools must be compatible. The students may also feel alienated from their high-school classmates. However, this type of collaboration between schools can also demystify the university experience and help students to perceive the continuity in their learning.

Granting Credit for Professional Activities

In most states, a teacher's license is no longer a lifelong authorization to teach. Most licenses must be renewed every three to five years, and teachers must provide documentation of professional learning for renewal. Usually, districts are in charge of certifying professional learning, which in some states must take the form of university credit. In all cases, university involvement can strengthen the professional work of teachers—and if university credits translate into a higher placement on a salary schedule, they can result in increased compensation as well.

Partnerships for Joint Projects

Schoolteachers and university faculty can collaborate on a variety of projects, such as formal or informal research studies or inquiries into the relative strengths of instructional approaches. A note of caution, however: some professors believe that they are the experts, and that they are sharing their knowledge with the teachers. These professors do not value the "wisdom of practice" of K–12 teachers, and regard themselves as the mentors. Such an arrangement is not a partnership; it does not feel like a partnership to the school-based educators any more than it does to the university faculty. True partnership involves a common agenda— a search for the best instructional method for a particular concept, for example—and a relationship that exploits the unique strengths of both K–12 teachers and professors. Every member of the partnership has a unique perspective to offer and should contribute in the manner best suited to her talents. There should be no senior or junior partners—only partners.

Summary

Only by building and strengthening their links with other institutions in the community can schools achieve their full mission. Local individuals and organizations—families and caregivers, public and private agencies, the business community, and colleges and universities—should not be regarded as competitors, but rather as partners in the education of the community's children.

➤ ➤ ➤

	Poor	Basic	Exemplary
		RUBRIC FOR LINKAGES BEYOND THE SCHOOL	
Communication	Communication with families, other educators, and the business community is nonexistent or minimal, or the information communicated is inaccurate.	The school's attempts to communicate with families, other educators, and the business community are partially successful, but misinformation or gaps in understanding persist.	The school's attempts to communicate with families, other educators, and the business community are fully successful. All members of the faculty are engaged in the communication effort, using all available means.
Collaboration with Public and Private Agencies	The school makes no attempts to collaborate with public or private agencies, resulting in gaps in or redundancies of services to the community.	The school collaborates somewhat with public and private agencies, but efforts are spotty and poorly organized, with mixed results.	The school collaborates extensively with public and private agencies, resulting in benefits for both the school and the agencies themselves.
Collaboration with the Business Community	The school makes no effort to forge partnerships with the business community and instead operates entirely on its own, even when collaboration would strengthen the school's program.	Some opportunities are provided for both students and teachers to collaborate with the business community, but the programs reach only a small percentage of either students or teachers.	The school has developed an extensive program of collaboration with the business community, resulting in valuable opportunities for both students and teachers.
Collaboration with Universities	The school does not collaborate with local universities, or the partnerships between them are not professionally rewarding.	The school makes a genuine attempt to form collaborations with local universities, but various obstacles prevent the efforts to pay dividends.	The school's collaboration with local universities is highly productive and professionally rewarding for both parties. The collaboration results in significant learning by all.

Programs

Aligned Curriculum

Assessment

Team Planning

Learning Support

Teaching

9

Aligned Curriculum

A school's curriculum refers to the expectations for student learning embodied in the school's learning objectives, programs, and course offerings, and translates the state or district content standards into a sequenced series of statements about what students will learn through their school experiences. The curriculum is not, for example, page 42 of the biology textbook. It is not even the whole textbook, or the end-of-year biology test. Rather, the curriculum is the vehicle through which educators make manifest their goals for student learning; it consists of the knowledge and skills that students learn through their study of biology, using the biology textbook and participating in the labs, which are then assessed through the end-of-course test.

Relationship to the Framework

Because the curriculum is composed of statements about what students will learn, it is the defining characteristic of the school's program. Everything is organized around the curriculum: the schedule must allow students to attend the right classes, the system of learning support must help students succeed in the curriculum, and teachers must form teams and plan their instruction to maximize student learning of the curriculum.

But what of the curriculum itself? How is it connected to the framework for school improvement presented in this book? How does it contribute to the successful learning of all students?

In the first place, the curriculum is organized and published. It is a public document; it is not kept private in the math department, say, or in a 3rd grade team. More importantly, the curriculum does not exist only in the mind of each teacher. If educators are serious about establishing a school in which all students are successful learners, the first step is to state unambiguously what they should learn. By writing this down in clear language, the school ensures that success is attainable by all students and is not a matter for teachers and students to negotiate privately.

Second, the curriculum should reflect high-level learning. Curriculum expectations should not be watered down in the misguided belief that an easy curriculum will be more accessible for students; instead they must reflect the belief that all students are capable of high-level learning. Of course, schools may offer a rigorous curriculum in many different ways. Many people think that a rigorous curriculum must be highly abstract and present information far from students' experiences. For example, 10th grade English teachers might introduce their students to George Bernard Shaw's *Pygmalion* by having them memorize facts about Shaw and about conditions in early 20th century London. Alternatively, however, they could ask students to imagine what it would take for someone growing up in their neighborhoods to pass as a princess, and from that to appreciate the challenge *Pygmalion* was addressing. This way, students would learn about Shaw's life and the conditions of early 20th century London as a result of their own investigations and engagement with the play, rather than having the information presented to them in an abstract (and boring) manner.

Similarly, a curriculum may be both rigorous and practical. For example, trigonometry may be presented using drawings of triangles and graphs of functions. This approach will be effective for many students. Others, however, might absorb the information more easily by exploring the subject in the context of designing airplane wings that will withstand stress. This latter approach will be particularly effective for students who would not be able to connect with a more abstract presentation. The content of both lessons is the same and the approaches are equally rigorous, but because the two approaches differ in their degree of abstraction, each appeals to different types of learners. A school's curriculum should be designed to engage the full range of students in the school.

The curriculum should also be organized in "chunks" small enough for students to experience success. If some subjects require prerequisite knowledge, the prerequisites should be listed in the curriculum. Students need to learn to write paragraphs before they can compose longer essays; they need to understand place value before they learn regrouping in addition and subtraction. In other words, students cannot be required to "fill in the blanks" on their own. The curriculum must permit students to build on their understanding as they move from simple to more complex topics.

Types of Curriculum Goals

A curriculum consists of a number of different types of goals for student learning, which include the following.

Knowledge

Every curriculum states what students should *know* upon completing their courses. Some knowledge is factual (important dates of the Civil War), whereas some is procedural (how to factor polynomials); some is low-level and true only by mutual consent ("$" as the symbol for dollar), and some is high-level, requiring extensive study (trends in the relationships between monarchs and parliaments throughout history). It is insufficient for students merely to *know* what the curriculum expects them to know; they should also *understand* it. Students should not only be able to recite the definition of "buoyancy" or "density," but also to explain these concepts in their own words and describe how they relate to other concepts, such as "sinking," "floating," or "displacement." Conceptual understanding should be the principal goal of the curriculum; when students understand facts and concepts, they can apply their knowledge to both existing and unfamiliar situations.

Thinking and Reasoning Skills

In addition to understanding concepts, students must be able to reason, draw conclusions, recognize patterns, discern trends, formulate and test hypotheses, compare and contrast different ideas, and interpret information in light of other findings. These skills are necessary for every citizen, not just the intellectual elite. Thinking and reasoning skills may be developed through, and serve to enrich, the regular curriculum.

Communication Skills

Equally critical to an educated person are the skills of communicating ideas to others through speaking, writing, visual representation, and the arts. Schools are dedicated to teaching students to express their ideas clearly and succinctly, to find the right words to convey a concept, and to organize their thoughts so that others can understand them. Students who can convey their ideas through visual representation such as charts, graphs, and diagrams possess a valuable tool with which to make and communicate meaning. The visual and performing arts—drawing and painting, sculpture, pottery, drama, music—afford students further opportunities to express their ideas. Many communication skills, such as reading and writing, are included in a school's core curriculum while others, such as the visual and performing arts, are available through elective courses or extracurricular offerings.

Social Skills

When business leaders—who after all employ students once they graduate—are asked what skills they value most in employees, they frequently emphasize the importance of social skills. In many such surveys, an ability to get along with others is at the top of the list, followed by thinking and reasoning skills and the ability and disposition to continue to learn. Business leaders report that they rarely fire employees for technical incompetence; much more frequently they let people go because they cannot get along with others. Children are not born with social skills; they must *learn* them, and school is an important place for them to do so.

Physical Skills

Physical skills abound in physical education, of course: skipping, kicking a ball, and playing volleyball are a few examples. But physical skills play a part in other areas of the curriculum as well, such as with handwriting, using a microscope correctly, playing a flute, or handling a paintbrush. Like other skills, physical skills must be learned and practiced before students can become proficient in them.

Aesthetics, Dispositions, and Ethics

In some communities, aesthetics, dispositions, and ethics are considered beyond the appropriate bounds of school learning. Most, however, consider at least some of them to be important to student learning and success. For example, the English curriculum includes poetry as a form to be not only analyzed, but also appreciated; similarly, math teachers teach their students the elegance of a simple approach when discussing how best to solve certain problems. Most schools attempt to instill in students perseverance, self-discipline, pride in work, and honesty. Goals such as these are rarely included as part of the written curriculum, but can provide a subtext for the choices teachers make when interacting with students.

Organizing the Curriculum

When developing the curriculum, educators should consider the following design issues.

Sequence

A well-organized curriculum will state its goals in a clear and coherent sequence. Complex ideas and skills should follow simpler ones, and students' abilities should be used in the service of further learning. Many topics will be revisited year after year in what is known as a "spiraling" curriculum: for example, fractions may be addressed in math classes every year from the 2nd to 8th

grade. Of course, student *goals* related to fractions will differ from grade to grade—from understanding the relationship of part to whole, for instance, to learning the proper notation for fractions, to comparing fractions of different sizes, to performing arithmetic operations on fractions. Although the topics are repeated, the curriculum goals themselves are not.

Another example of the spiraling curriculum is U.S. history: while the subject may be taught in both the 8th and 11th grades, the learning expected of students in each is considerably different. As juniors in high school, students bring a more developed historical and political sense to their study of history than they could have in middle school; they are now better able to appreciate the nuances of history, and are capable of imagining hypothetical situations and their possible consequences.

Required vs. Elective

Elements of the curriculum for elementary students are typically consistent: they are all required, and all students in the school are expected to demonstrate that they have learned to read and write to, for instance, the standards of the 5th grade curriculum. The situation begins to change in middle school, where some of the curriculum is consistent and required for all students, while other portions are optional.

The distinction between mandatory and elective courses is most critical in high schools, which are typically required by the state's department of education to establish graduation requirements. These might consist, for example, of four credits in English; three credits each of science, mathematics, and social studies; two credits of world language;

and so on. Beyond these requirements, all other courses in the high school are elective, and students select them according to their own preferences and post graduation plans. In addition, high school educators must determine which course may be used to satisfy the different graduation requirements. For example, does journalism "count" as one of the English credits?

Coordination and Integration

Teachers and curriculum specialists tend to think of subjects as distinct bodies of knowledge requiring discrete ways of "knowing." Although it is true that each discipline has its own structure and methods of inquiry, topics can be either coordinated or integrated across disciplines, thus enhancing the power of both. For example, many schools decide to teach both U.S. history and American literature in the 11th grade, so that students can have the benefit of each to enrich the other: history puts literature in context, while literature provides a window on the culture of each historical period. Similarly, the reasoning skills of comparing and contrasting must be developed and practiced using real content, which can be from one of the disciplines that is part of the knowledge to be acquired. Coordination and integration of curriculum is not only more efficient than treating each subject separately, but also vastly improves the quality of learning.

Curriculum Design

Most curriculum experts adopt a "design-down" approach when designing a school or district curriculum; that is, they "begin with the end in mind" and design the curriculum backwards from there.

What this means, in a practical sense, is that when students are asked to demonstrate their knowledge and skill on a high-stakes assessment test, educators must begin their curriculum work with the content of that assessment, and work from there. They must ensure that, whatever else is offered in the curriculum, students at least have access to the learning on which they will be assessed.

In developing curriculum at the school or district level, educators follow clearly defined steps that are designed to link the local curriculum to state and district content standards, while at the same time including some "local flavor" in their offerings. The educators typically employ a process in which those with the most expertise (namely, the teachers of the different disciplines at different levels) make the important decisions. Their work is usually coordinated by a district administrator and enhanced by outside experts, such as a professor from a local university. But the teachers make the essential curriculum decisions.

Developing Program Goals

Program goals are broad statements of *what* students are expected to learn in each of the disciplines, and are a function of the district's broader educational goals, graduation requirements, and the need for balance among different types of goals. These goals may have to do with knowledge, thinking and communication skills, and even affective skills.

Program goals should include a list of the most critical knowledge and skills that all students are expected to learn in each major discipline. This should not be a long list—probably fewer than 10 items—so each item will necessarily refer to a broad area of learning. English program goals might include: "Graduates can write effectively for a variety of purposes and audiences," or "Graduates can analyze literature of different genres from different historical periods and cultural traditions."

Defining Courses

The term "course" here refers to a collection of content that is best studied together, usually over a one-year period. Thus, one year of science at the elementary level is considered a course, as is Biology I in high school.

Program areas usually consist of several related courses, frequently one for each year of school, with a few additional electives at the high-school level. In math, therefore, the program (divided into seven or eight yearlong courses, because it would take most students that long to complete) might consist of Basic Math, Algebra I, Geometry, Algebra II, Trigonometry, Math Analysis, Calculus, Consumer Math, Business Math, and Math Applications.

Some creativity is possible when designing curriculum, of course. For example, the traditional sequence of science courses in many high schools is biology, chemistry, and physics, followed by an elective advanced course for seniors. Some schools, however, take an "integrated" approach to science, whereby aspects of biology, chemistry, and physics are all taught in each of the three years. Many scientists recommend this approach, believing that it better reflects new developments and the gradual merging of the disciplines. There are trade-offs to this type of program, however. The more nontraditional a curriculum is, the more it will have to be explained to individuals and institutions, potential employers, and colleges and universities. Also, the more unusual a curriculum is,

the more difficult it is to identify instructional materials. But when educators feel strongly about the benefits of designing their courses in a nontraditional manner, they will find ways to meet these challenges. At this stage in the planning process, end-of-course assessments will be defined (this issue is further addressed in Chapter 10: Assessment).

Dividing Courses into Units

Once the courses have been decided, the major topics for each of the units need to be determined. If it has been decided that every course will have 12 units and that the 6th and 12th units will be devoted to review and synthesis, then the topics of the remaining 10 units must be determined. In a U.S. history course, for example, one unit might be called "Early Exploration," another "Life in Colonial America," and so on.

What constitutes a unit will depend on how many units there are and on how long they are intended to last; the content of each unit will be determined by the nature of the subject and by the natural breaks in the sequence. If some units are prerequisites for others, these relationships should be determined during the division of the course into units.

At this stage in the planning process, courses may also be coordinated across the disciplines: for example, the English department might decide to teach a unit on "Persuasion in the Political Essay" to coincide with a history unit on the American Revolution.

Planning Units

The final step in curriculum design is the detailed planning of each unit. This is typically done by teachers, either individually or in teams. At this point, the specific learning objectives, materials, instructional activities, standards, and assessments are determined. This stage of the design process is what many people think of when they hear about teachers "writing curriculum," although as is evident from our discussion thus far, it follows an extensive series of prior activities.

Summary

A curriculum in a school organized for high-level learning by all students must first of all be rigorous, and should demand high levels of cognitive engagement from students; in other words, it should require them to *think*. But the curriculum need not be highly abstract: understanding may be developed through in-depth exploration of topics to which the students can relate. The curriculum should also be

➤ Complete, with all the prerequisites identified;

➤ Public and known to all, including students, parents, the public, and the business community;

➤ Sequenced and aligned to ensure successful engagement by all students; and

➤ Supported by materials that permit students to engage with it in a meaningful way.

The curriculum is a school's description of what it will teach its students; it gives meaning to the school's academic goals. Although the district is in charge of many curriculum decisions, some are reserved for individual schools, teams of teachers, or teachers working on their own.

➤   ➤   ➤

	Poor	Basic	Exemplary
RUBRIC FOR ALIGNED CURRICULUM			
Standards	The curriculum bears no relation to state or district content standards or to the school's goals for student learning.	The curriculum's connection to state or district content standards and the school's goals for student learning is uneven: some items are clearly connected, whereas others do not appear linked at all.	The curriculum is clearly connected to state or district content standards and the school's goals for student learning.
Content	Curriculum expectations are expressed primarily as activities rather than as learning goals, or represent only a few types of objectives. Curriculum outcomes are not coordinated or integrated across disciplines, even when opportunities clearly exist to do so.	The curriculum reflects a mixture of goals, activities, and different types of content. A few opportunities for coordination and integration are exploited, but others are not.	Curriculum expectations represent various suitable types of content, and are stated clearly as learning goals. Where appropriate, curriculum expectations are coordinated or integrated across different disciplines.
Offerings	Courses and extracurricular offerings are only partially related to the stated learning goals; many students have little or no opportunity to acquire the knowledge and skills in the curriculum.	Courses and extracurricular offerings offer most students at least one opportunity to acquire and demonstrate the knowledge and skills specified in the curriculum.	Courses and extracurricular offerings offer all students multiple opportunities to acquire and demonstrate the knowledge and skills specified in the school's goals.
Sequence & Organization	The curriculum's sequence is disorganized, with little or no coherence among learning goals or reference to students' developmental levels and prior learning.	The curriculum's sequence is uneven, the learning goals are not entirely coherent, and some reference is made to students' developmental levels or their prior learning.	The curriculum's sequence is rational, with more complex ideas building on simpler ones, respecting students' developmental levels and prior learning.

10

Assessment

A school's system of assessment permits educators to ascertain how much their students are learning. Indeed, assessments provide an operational definition of curriculum goals: it is by answering the question "What could students do if they knew X?" that teachers and curriculum specialists determine what their curriculum statements really mean. In combination, curriculum and assessment fully define what students will learn; where curriculum lays out what students *will* learn, assessments show what they *have* learned. It would be reasonable to regard assessments as simply part of the curriculum planning effort—one more element of a well-designed curriculum. However, because of the complexity of the topic, and because of its importance given the current educational focus on accountability, it warrants a separate examination.

As I explained in Chapter 9, there are many different kinds of learning goals, such as knowledge, reasoning skills, etc. Assessment methodologies must be appropriate to the types of goals being assessed. Although short-answer or multiple-choice questions might be suitable for goals related to knowledge, essay questions or oral presentations are more appropriate for measuring communication or reasoning skills. Some dispositional goals—such as persistence or aesthetic appreciation—are virtually impossible to assess formally; in these cases, anecdotal accounts may have to suffice.

Relationship to the Framework

In a school committed to the successful learning of all students, the approach to assessment must be completely transparent to both students and their parents. There is no place for secrecy or mystery; students must know *in advance* what they will need to do to demonstrate their learning.

In addition, students should have multiple assessment methods available to them to show their learning. For example, a student might not be able to write numerals fast enough to complete a multiplication test in the required time, and yet knows the facts cold. In such a case, the teacher might ask that student to answer questions verbally in order to assess the student's mastery of the content.

Assessments should never be used as punishments, but *should* be used to validate learning. They may be used diagnostically, of course, when used in a formative manner. But even when used summatively, assessments (and student preparation for them) can guide learning. Students should have a sufficiently clear understanding of what to expect from a test to confidently say, "Ask me anything—I'm ready!"

Assessments should not force students to compete against one another; any "competition" should be between students and their own prior performance. In a school working toward high-level learning for all students, a good performance is always cause for celebration, by students as well as teachers. It is not only the "top 5" students who receive an "A;" any student who exceeds the standard established for an "A" should receive one. In other words, students are not trying to be better than others in the class; they are trying to be as good as they can. This orientation sets up an entirely different climate within the class.

Purposes of Assessment

There are many purposes of assessment, including some that are only tangential to the interests of school staff for detailed instructional planning. For example, most states have established assessments to determine how well students measure up to state content standards, the results of which may be used to hold students accountable for their learning as well as to evaluate the effectiveness of a school's instructional program. Such standardized assessments can play a role in a school's approach to improving student learning, but because they are not designed by teachers, I will not address them further in this chapter.

Degree of Success on Standards

Well-designed assessments can inform educators about the degree to which students are meeting state or district content standards. This is not trivial information, and can in fact provide schools with critical feedback about the effectiveness of their programs. Assessment results are valuable not only as one-shot data, but can also reveal much about trends and patterns, allowing educators to set improvement goals from one year to the next.

Feedback to Students

Assessment results can provide valuable feedback to students on their progress. When aligned with important curriculum goals, assessments results offer students an indication of where they should put their energies, and to what aspects of the curriculum they should pay closer attention.

Feedback to students can be formative or summative. The results of summative assessments may be incorporated into grades; formative assessments, on the other hand, are an integral part of the instructional sequence and are used exclusively to guide future learning.

Educators should keep in mind that students themselves can play an important role in the assessment process, particularly when the evaluations are formative. In addition to learning the assessment criteria and the methods teachers use to evaluate their work, students can assess themselves or their peers, and can use the results to plan future efforts. By using assessments in this manner, students are empowered to take charge of their own learning. (This issue is further addressed in Chapter 13: Teaching.)

Feedback to Parents

Parents are keenly interested in the progress of their students. For most parents, the concern is general: "How is he doing?" "Is she on track?" Primarily, parents want to know that their children are making reasonable progress, and how they can facilitate their learning. Students themselves can play an important part in explaining their progress to their parents; this is one of the wonderful uses of student portfolios. When students collect samples of their work together in one place and show them to their parents, they are taking increased ownership and pride both in the work and in the learning for which the work provides evidence.

Analysis of Instruction

Teachers often use assessments to determine their own strengths and weaknesses as well as what aspects of their instruction they need to emphasize. After reviewing student performance on a unit test, for example, a teacher might notice that many of his students simply didn't grasp a certain concept. Although the reasons for the students' lack of understanding may not be clear—the instruction might have been muddled, or perhaps the students didn't try hard enough—the teacher has to decide what to do next.

Assessment Methodologies

Many different types of assessments can be designed and used at the school site. They may be used commonly across a district, and they may reflect the district curriculum, but at least some are developed for use in the classroom and school.

Tests

When taking tests, students typically work individually, under time restrictions, and with no access to outside resources (except during "open-book" tests); these three characteristics together create what are known as "testing conditions." There are two fundamental types of tests: "select" and "constructed response." Both are used by the vast majority of teachers.

In select tests, students choose the correct answer from a provided list. Types of select tests include multiple-choice, matching, and true-or-false. Many teachers use select-test items for the same reason that commercial test publishers use them: they are quick to correct. Yet despite being effective for assessing factual and even some procedural knowledge, select tests are not usually good for measuring conceptual understanding or communication skills. In addition, many teachers find select-test questions very difficult to construct: the answers provided must be unambiguously correct without being too obvious; incorrect answers (or "distracters") must be clearly wrong, yet still somewhat plausible. As a result, teachers rarely derive all the information they could from such tests. However, because they are an efficient way to assess a broad range of student knowledge and skill, educators will probably always use select tests of some sort.

In constructed-response tests, students supply or construct their own answers to questions; examples include fill-in-the-blank and short-essay tests. These types of assessments typically require students to know more about a subject than do select tests. Constructed-response test items are usually easy to construct, but harder to correct. Essay questions must be phrased clearly enough that students know what information they're supposed to supply: if a question is ambiguously stated and the students perform poorly, neither teacher nor student will be able to state with any confidence that they did not know the content. Even when essay questions are stated clearly, answers can vary tremendously; as a result, essays are much harder to grade than are fill-in-the-blanks questions, which usually have a single correct answer. Indeed, most teachers find that they need a scoring rubric to evaluate student essays.

Most tests that teachers create are a combination of select and constructed-response items. A history test, for example, might consist of 20 multiple-choice items worth 4 points apiece and two short essays worth 10 points each.

Products

Another type of assessment that teachers can use is a "product" assessment, of which there are two types: written and physical.

Written products may take a variety of forms; examples include term papers, short plays, lab reports, newspaper articles, and letters to public officials. Depending on how the assignments are structured, written products can reveal a great deal about levels of student understanding and skill. As with essay questions, teachers usually use rubrics to evaluate written products, and teachers must make their evaluative criteria known to the students. The principal difference between written products and essay tests is that the latter (unlike the former) are typically completed under testing conditions.

Some disciplines use physical products, such as dioramas, sculptures, or photographs, to assess student work. In a few subjects, such as fine arts, physical products may be the best evidence of student learning. Naturally, teachers should evaluate these using rubrics.

Many teachers use products to assess student learning. Most science projects, for instance, are a combination of physical product (a model of the water cycle, for example) and written product (a description of how the water cycle works).

Performance

Students can also demonstrate their knowledge and skill through performance, of which there are two basic types: structured and spontaneous.

Structured performances are responses to assignments, such as oral presentations and poetry recitations. Students can conduct their performances in groups, as when creating a skit, staging a panel discussion, or participating on the debate team. In all cases, is essential that students know how their performances will be evaluated. If the culture of the class permits it, students can even be part of the assessment process, particularly if the assessments are meant to be formative: for example, students can provide feedback to their peers on how clearly they recited their poems or on the cogency of their oral presentations.

Spontaneous student performances occur independent of structured assignments and form the basis of many teachers' anecdotal records. A teacher who has been emphasizing skills of group work, for example, can best assess her students' grasp of the skills by watching them work in groups. Spontaneous performance is rarely part of any plan for summative assessment, but can be enormously valuable to teachers.

Naturally, some of these assessment methodologies are more suitable for certain types of learning goals than for others: whereas select tests are adequate measures of factual or procedural knowledge, for example, constructed-response tests or written products are more accurate gauges of conceptual knowledge or thinking skills. Some cases are particularly clear-cut: to assess writing skills, for instance, nothing short of a writing sample will do. And physical skills must be assessed through performance. Because a school's assessments in effect define its learning goals, decisions about types of assessment to employ must convey the right messages: if complex, high-level learning is desired, then the assessments must demand complex, high-level performance. It is not sufficient to *claim* to want high-level learning; educators must also assess the learning using low-level methods.

Designing Assessments

My comments on assessment design are based on the assumption that teachers in a given grade level and discipline teach a common curriculum. Although each may bring her own perspective to the content and use different instructional strategies, all want their students to learn the same skills and knowledge in 6th grade language arts, for instance, or in algebra. Because they teach a common curriculum, these teachers give the same summative assessments to their students at the end of the year or semester. This consistency ensures that assessments will convey critical information to the teachers who inherit these students in the next grade or in a related course.

Assessment design consists of the following steps.

Step 1: Arriving at Consensus on Content

First, teachers in a given grade level and discipline must agree on the content of their course; they should determine, in other words, what students should know and be able to do at the end of the year or semester. At this stage, educators need not discuss particular topics or materials, although if they wish to they may; first and foremost they should ask themselves: What is the *learning*? What do we want our students to be able to do? In a 2nd grade reading course, the answer might be: "To predict the outcome of a story," or "To be able to tell fairy tales from fables." If a school or district has engaged in a systematic curriculum planning effort, this step will have been addressed as "defining courses."

Clearly, teachers cannot test all that is important. Because instructional goals are far broader than even the most ambitious evaluation plan can capture, educators must choose only the most critical content to assess. This is a matter for professional consensus: of all the content that students are exposed to in biology, for example, which is most critical that the students demonstrate they have learned?

Step 2: Determining Appropriate Methodology

When educators say students should understand a particular concept, what exactly do they mean? Do they mean that students should be able to repeat a definition that they have memorized by rote, or to explain the concept in their own words? Do they mean that students should be able to apply the concept to a new and unfamiliar context? Assessment design will depend on the answers to these questions. Educators must arrive at a consensus about what assessment methods to use and about what the students will actually be asked to do to demonstrate their knowledge and skill.

Step 3: Developing Assessment Rubrics

The next step in assessment design is to determine, for each of the essential criteria, what different levels of student performance will look like. What are the respective characteristics of poor, adequate, and exemplary performances? These conversations typically result in scoring rubrics with clearly articulated levels of performance. These rubrics must be shared with students— indeed, some teachers find that students can contribute to their development. Students who are involved in developing or using scoring rubrics

internalize the standards of excellence and know how to achieve them.

Step 4: Setting Performance Standards and Benchmarks

Teachers must next agree on what constitutes acceptable student performance on an assessment. By reviewing actual samples of student work, teachers determine which would meet their standards and which would not, and why. These samples are known as "benchmarks" or "benchmark performances." Once teachers have decided which ones meet their standards, they can show them to students to help them see standards in action.

Summary

A school's assessments serve as an operational definition of the curriculum; they state unambiguously what students need to do to demonstrate their knowledge and skill. As such, assessments can serve to structure and guide the daily work of students and teachers. Assessments may be used for many different purposes by students, teachers, and schools; they can provide formative information about student learning to guide future studies, and can certify mastery of a segment of the curriculum, thus enabling students to move on to more challenging work. By stating publicly the requirements of the curriculum, assessments go a long way towards ensuring student success in that curriculum.

➤　➤　➤

RUBRIC FOR ASSESSMENT			
	Poor	**Basic**	**Exemplary**
Alignment with the Curriculum	The curriculum either has no commonly used assessments or the assessments are not aligned to the curriculum goals.	School staff has attempted to establish common assessments, which are partially aligned to the curriculum goals.	The faculty has established common assessments that are completely aligned to the curriculum goals.
Assessment Methodologies	The assessment methodologies used are poorly suited to the curriculum goals.	The assessment methodologies used are partially suited to the curriculum goals.	The assessment methodologies used are completely appropriate to the curriculum goals.
Criteria and Standards	Performance standards are unclear and have not been shared with students.	Performance standards are fairly clear and some are shared with students.	Performance standards are completely clear and have all been shared with students.
Interpretation of Student Work	Teachers interpret student work in highly idiosyncratic and inconsistent ways, making it impossible to draw any conclusions from the results.	Teachers attempt to interpret student work consistently, but results are uneven.	Teachers interpret student work consistently, enabling them to draw important conclusions from their analysis.

11

Team Planning

Most teachers in schools committed to improving student learning are organized into teams of some sort, such as grade-level or "family" teams in elementary schools, "houses" in middle schools, and departments or schools-within-a-school in high schools. The details of how each team's internal planning is accomplished is a function, first of all, of that overall school organization. But once that general school organization is determined, there is still much detailed planning to be done, and it can only be done by the individuals involved. For example, when teams are organized, the manner in which their members work together is greatly influenced by the master schedule. Of course, some teachers believe that they are most effective working on their own rather than in a team. Although this could be true for some individuals, most educators have experienced the benefits of teamwork and joint planning for professional camaraderie and student learning: when teachers work together to plan and implement the curriculum everyone seems to benefit. As with everything else about schools, there are exceptions to the general rule; in certain situations—the case of a middle school teacher charged with producing the school musical, for example—opportunities for collaboration are limited. But for the most part, team planning works to the advantage of students and staff.

Relationship to the Framework

The ultimate goal of teachers working together to plan the day-to-day instructional program is for all students to successfully learn the curriculum. The success of each teacher on the 3rd grade team, 7th grade house, or science department is a direct function of the success of *all* 3rd graders, 7th graders, or science students. Teachers in team arrangements cannot think of only certain students as their "own." Likewise, teachers mustn't consider that they have "taught" chemistry if many of their students haven't successfully learned the required material; in such a situation, the program has not been successful.

The mechanisms described in this chapter allow teachers to ensure that all of their students gain the knowledge and skills they need to succeed in the curriculum. Teachers who work as a team can exercise greater flexibility when forming instructional groups than they could working on their own, as students in any group have many different levels of knowledge and skill. If four teachers work together to teach 100 3rd graders math, the teachers can continually subdivide the students into different instructional groups as their learning needs evolve.

Team teaching should build on the individual strengths of the educators involved. A teacher who knows a lot about poetry, for example, might be able to structure a poetry unit for use by the entire team. Another teacher might be especially well versed in science, and thus could serve as a resource to the rest of the team (by designing activities and locating materials, for instance).

When teachers plan instruction together, they take account of the curriculum and assessments, structure the schedule and instructional groups, and deploy the teachers to ensure that all students are successful. In addition, such teachers know that they can use the learning support system for additional help when needed.

Background of Team Planning

It is virtually impossible to separate the benefits of collaborative planning from those of collegial professional development. Yet although these two practices reinforce each other, they are functionally distinct: when teachers plan instruction together, their focus is on the continuous improvement of student learning; when they come together to improve instruction, on the other hand, their focus is on enhancing their own skills, and their work together may or may not involve the learning outcomes of specific students. Although student performance often improves as a result, the *goal* of collaboration for professional development is to increase the "intellectual capital" of teachers, not students. Team planning, as described in this chapter, concerns the efforts of teachers working together to enhance the learning of students.

As they engage in team planning, educators should recognize that there are two distinct areas of the curriculum: skill areas (reading, math, language arts) and concept areas (science and social studies). In general, skill areas are foundational—they are essential for success in the concept areas. Virtually all state and district testing programs assess students in the basic skills, whereas large-scale testing of the concept areas is relatively rare. Most people consider skill areas more important than concept areas, at least up to a certain minimum standard. They argue that if students cannot learn to read, write, and do basic math, then everything else is immaterial. When considering team planning, then, it is useful to determine whether the same issues apply to both the skill and concept areas.

There are important prerequisite relationships between the different topics in the skill areas; later topics will not make sense if the earlier content has not yet been learned. Failure to understand a particular topic in the skill areas holds serious consequences for the future success of students: a child who has not fully mastered 3rd grade math is likely to have trouble with math in the 4th grade. Even worse, such a student will probably start down the long and discouraging road of school failure, struggling at first to succeed but eventually giving up altogether. Elaborate compensation and avoidance strategies will follow, and only an alert teacher will even recognize the signs of a student's lack of understanding. Some students in this situation come to rely increasingly on their memories, learning as much as they can by rote, but without really understanding the concepts. Furthermore, because these students know that their memories are not trustworthy, they come to feel increasingly vulnerable and alienated towards school.

It is not surprising, then, that the many adults who live all their lives with what is called "math anxiety" are those who failed to understand something years ago and then, inevitably, failed at the next step and went on failing. It is likely that such failure was due to a combination of age-grade groupings and grade-level curriculum, and could have been avoided through careful team planning.

A lockstep approach to instruction does not serve advanced students well, either. Students who are forced to sit through lessons when they already know the material can easily become bored and disruptive, and may conclude that they don't have to apply themselves very hard in order to succeed. This attitude can be difficult to change in later years when the students encounter topics that require them to commit all their intellectual energy; if school learning has always come easily to them, they may give up at the first sign of challenge. Hence, an important purpose of team planning is to provide a challenging instructional setting for advanced students, as well as a setting where those who learn with more difficulty can succeed.

Characteristics of Successful Team Planning

Team planning activities that address basic skills are somewhat different from those that deal with concept skills. Team planning for instruction in the basic skills should ensure that

➤ Each student is placed accurately in the curriculum. That is, given an established curriculum aligned to the state or district's content standards, "where" in that curriculum is each student? Is every nine-year-old, for example, ready to learn the 4th grade curriculum? Or are some still work-ing their way through the content of the 3rd grade curriculum and others ready for the topics included in the 5th grade curriculum?

➤ Students are assigned to appropriate instructional groups based on their placement in the curriculum.

➤ The system allows for students to be reassigned to different instructional groups as their learning needs change.

To gain maximum benefit from team planning in the concept skills, educators working together should

> ➤ Organize the curriculum around large themes to help students investigate major topics in depth and identify patterns and trends.
> ➤ Integrate basic skills throughout the curriculum. For example, once students have learned the skills of expository writing, they can hone these skills by writing essays for social studies class or science.
> ➤ Integrate critical reasoning skills—such as classification, comparison-contrast, pattern recognition, and separation and control of variables—throughout the curriculum. The skill of overlapping classification, for instance, may be taught and practiced in science, then applied in other contexts.

One prerequisite for successful team planning, particularly in the basic skill areas, is a well-developed system of assessment. In order to ascertain the degree to which each student understands the curriculum, schools must have comprehensive methods in place to assess and monitor student mastery of curriculum objectives. Such a system is critical at schools with a high transience rate: because some students may not attend the school for very long, it is essential to make the most of every instructional opportunity.

Requirements of Successful Team Planning

To be successful, team planning must be accompanied by the attitudes and arrangements described below.

Staff Commitment to the Process

Teachers will abandon joint planning unless they can see that it is effective. The last thing teachers need is another meeting; if they believe joint planning is just taking time away from their own work—for which they have too little time as it is—they will not devote the necessary time or energy to the effort. Joint planning must yield improved outcomes for students and more efficient work for teachers if it is to be sustained. An ineffective joint effort can reinforce a negative professional culture: teachers might interpret a school's emphasis on joint planning as merely one more top-down reform with little connection to their own lives.

Teachers must make the time commitment necessary for team planning to succeed. No team can operate successfully if members are late for meetings or decline to participate. Team planning is hard work, and although it is likely to yield better results for students, the staff involved must be willing to invest the time and energy to make the team function smoothly.

Acceptance of the Team Concept

Some individuals like teams in theory, but have difficulty relinquishing their independence in practice. Worse, they may manipulate the assignment of students to instructional groups so they teach the least challenging students. Such teachers are more concerned about their own convenience than they are about the success of the students.

Teachers who embrace the concept of a team, on the other hand, welcome opportunities to contribute their skills to the group. If this means teaching a few very challenging students, then they do it. These teachers acknowledge the success of the team as a whole, not of themselves as individuals; they are, to use the cliché, "team players."

Use of Teachers' Strengths

When teachers work together, they can capitalize on one another's strengths for planning, instruction, or both. This mutual assistance can be especially useful in elementary school, where teachers are typically asked to teach eight different subjects by themselves. No one teacher can be an expert in all eight subjects, but all have areas of relative strength; teachers working together can take advantage of their different areas of expertise.

Time

Team planning is probably more time consuming than individual planning. Of course, teachers don't plan instruction together to save time, but to offer their students superior instruction. Successful teams find a good time to meet and stick to it. In the most convenient arrangements, team members share the same planning time—they might, for example, devote one meeting a week for collaborative work. Common planning time is not always possible, however, and time must be found elsewhere in the schedule.

Activities of Successful Team Planning

Joint Curriculum and Assessment Planning

Team planning can succeed only within the context of a clear curriculum and aligned assessments. A major team planning activity is to determine the shared curriculum and to decide how student learning of that curriculum should be

assessed. (These matters are discussed more fully in Chapter 9: Aligned Curriculum and Chapter 10: Assessment.)

Maintaining Flexible Instructional Groups Within the Master Schedule

Among an instructional team's most important activities is to create and maintain flexible instructional groups. In traditional school structures, there is often a gap between what students are ready to learn and what the school is prepared to provide, particularly in the basic-skills areas of the curriculum. Each team is responsible for determining the most appropriate instructional group for each of its students. Most teams use thorough and ongoing student assessments to determine their students' learning needs, and are open to reassignments that will benefit the students. When this flexibility is combined with learning support resources, the result can be powerful.

Sharing Instructional Strategies

Every teacher can learn from colleagues. Teaching is so complex that there is no such thing as perfection; practice can always be improved. Most educators recognize that enormous expertise exists within their schools' walls; the challenge is how to liberate that expertise so that all teachers can benefit.

Although veteran teachers almost certainly have a more extensive repertoire of skills to draw from than do novice teachers, the latter may have learned cutting-edge instructional approaches in college with which older colleagues would be unfamiliar. By sharing strategies, teachers help to promote a culture of professional inquiry in the school and to forge a common purpose among team members as they cultivate and refine their approaches to instruction.

Integration and Coordination

The school program is greatly strengthened when teachers integrate and coordinate topics in the curriculum. For example, teachers of 11th grade English may decide to make U.S. literature the focus of their course, knowing that 11th graders are studying U.S. history. Students enrolled in physics need to be familiar with concepts from Algebra II and trigonometry; the science and math teachers should coordinate to ensure that any such prerequisites are covered in one course before they are assumed in another. And if a certain level of proficiency in math, for example, is a prerequisite for success in physics, students themselves should be apprised of this, so that they may plan their studies accordingly.

More extensive integration of topics is possible as well. A team of teachers could decide to teach the curriculum through a single, unifying theme: for example, a group of teachers in a middle school might decide to organize much of their instruction around the theme of "walls and bridges." The teachers would probably determine the theme by forging a link with the required social studies curriculum for their grade level. Once determined, the theme can affect the work students do across the disciplines: they can explore the physical properties of walls, for example, in science class; the Berlin Wall and Great Wall of China in history; and the metaphoric walls of race and class divisions in social studies. Such thematic study, although not always possible, lends coherence to, and heightens the meaning of, many students' school experiences.

Summary

Team planning is a direct consequence of the organization of the school and reflects the school's team structure. The manner in which teachers make critical decisions depends on their commitment to the success of every student: when teachers make decisions wisely and flexibly, instructional planning proceeds efficiently; as a result, teachers can be sure that the students arriving in class are prepared to be successful.

➤ ➤ ➤

	RUBRIC FOR TEAM PLANNING		
	Poor	**Basic**	**Exemplary**
Staff Commitment	Teachers do not commit fully to the team planning process: for example, they are late for meetings, take credit for other people's ideas, or manipulate the assignment of students.	Teachers make a partial commitment to the team planning process; they participate in planning sessions, but do not give them their full energy.	Teachers make a complete commitment to the team planning process, participating fully and enthusiastically, and yielding individual interests to those of the team.
Quality of Decisions	The team planning process yields no decisions or poor ones regarding curriculum and assessment, coordination and integration, and student assignments to instructional groups.	Some decisions made through the team planning process are of high quality while others are not; the decision-making process is uneven.	Decisions made through the team planning process are of uniformly high quality.
Sharing Instructional Strategies	Few teachers contribute to the dialogue regarding improved instructional strategies. The team has not developed a culture of sharing to improve teaching techniques.	Some teachers participate in sharing instructional strategies, while others hold back. Although the culture of sharing has been established, the full benefits have not been realized.	Teachers enthusiastically share instructional strategies to enhance their own practice and that of their teammates. Sharing results in improved teaching techniques by all team members and enhanced student learning.
Coordination and Integration of Instruction	Teachers work entirely independently, without coordinating or integrating instruction between them.	Teachers find opportunities to coordinate their efforts; however, no integration is attempted.	Teachers create extensive opportunities for students to integrate their learning across disparate curricular areas.

12

Learning Support

A school's learning support system provides extra assistance to students who need it to make satisfactory progress in their learning. The system is a safety net for students, preventing them from falling through the cracks of the school program; it should not permit any student to fail.

Although a well-designed learning support program is most critical for students at risk of school failure, others can benefit as well: teachers, for example, are served by having somewhere to turn when they can't meet the needs of some of their students; they can enlist the assistance of colleagues, who might suggest alternate instructional approaches. Students who don't need extra help can also benefit from a learning support system, which keeps teachers from directing all of their energies toward the few who need additional assistance. Even advanced students can benefit: although struggling students should be the system's first clients, any spare capacity can be directed toward the needs of students who are not being adequately challenged in the regular program, such as those typically identified as "gifted." Thus the learning support program supports the learning of all students within a school, ensuring that they are both successful and challenged, as well as supporting the work of teachers.

Relationship to the Framework

As with every other aspect of school improvement, the learning support system must support the school's goals for student

99

learning, reflect the school's belief structures, and be consistent with current research on teaching and learning. These matters are embodied in the philosophy of learning support.

Learning support programs reflect a school's commitment to the successful learning of all students, as well as the belief that all students are natural learners—that any difficulties they encounter are probably short-term and can be addressed with little fanfare. This approach differs considerably from the prevailing view in many remedial and special education programs, where students are labeled and treated differently from their peers. Teachers in these programs may even refer to their students, in their presence, as "Title I students," or some other designation that sets them apart.

In contrast, a learning support program operates on the premise that just as all human beings are natural learners, all individuals may encounter difficulty in their learning. Of course, this does not mean that those having trouble learning are any less able or committed to learning than their peers; virtually no one is equally capable in all aspects of learning, and everyone is likely to run into rough spots from time to time. The goal of a learning support system is to extend extra help to any student who needs it, no questions asked, and without stigmatizing that individual. Assistance must be available in a timely fashion, without anyone—student or teacher—having to jump through a lot of hoops.

A learning support program, then, is designed to support both teachers and students in their work, to enable all students to be successful and challenged in the school's curriculum. It acknowledges that some students need extra time and support in order to learn, and recognizes that all students, regardless of their general abilities, may need additional assistance from time to time; it can also support the learning of advanced students when the capacity permits it. The learning support system is one important manifestation of a school's success orientation, and sends a message that failure is not tolerated.

Dangers of Learning Support

Educators planning to institute a system of learning support should be aware of the obstacles, primarily mental, that stand in their way. These are briefly described below.

The Labeling Phenomenon

The idea that learning difficulties reflect inherent problems in students is central to special education legislation. Most diagnostic procedures—which since the passage of PL94-142 have become long and elaborate—consist of searching for what is "wrong" with students, effectively discounting the possibility that the educational setting itself might be deficient. The unstated assumption of these diagnoses is that the school has discharged its responsibilities adequately and that any unsatisfactory progress must be due to some shortcoming or handicap in the student.

This problem is well illustrated by the very term "learning disability," which has come to refer broadly to learning difficulties that cannot be adequately explained by low IQ or any other recognizable handicap. Students so labeled simply do not perform up to their presumed potential, and are therefore assumed to have some invisible disability. Again, the problem—which educators can't even identify—is presumed to originate in the student rather than the school. In practice, many students who are classified as "learning disabled" do not differ significantly from other low-performing students who are not so categorized. Unfortunately, the availability of funds for the learning disabled, along with a lack of consensus as to what the term even means, has motivated educators to categorize as many students as possible as disabled.

Consequences of Labeling

The current situation, in which funds are available for students who qualify for assistance under the categorical programs, creates a dilemma for schools that want to use this money for their learning support programs. Much of the problem has to do with the labeling of students as "disabled," which can undermine the effectiveness of the programs the funds are intended to help.

Teacher Expectations and Behavior

When students have been classified and labeled as "special education," "Title I," or "remedial" students, teachers' expectations are inevitably diminished. Even if teachers embrace the success orientation described in this book, they may wonder whether their "special" students can actually live up to the expectations of success for all students. Abundant research has confirmed the devastating effect that teachers' lowered expectations can have on students: they can become self-fulfilling prophecies (Rosenthal & Jacobson, 1968; Mortimore, 1991). In other words, students who are labeled as "disabled" perform poorly in part because they are expected to do so—thereby confirming the teachers' initial low expectations.

Student Self-Confidence

Students who are labeled as needing special assistance know that the label suggests they are inferior. Calling students "special" cannot erase their greatest fear: being different from other students. As children grow older, they need more and more to be accepted by their peers; the more they are treated differently from their classmates, the greater their fear that there is something "wrong" with them, and the more their confidence is undermined—especially toward academic work.

At the same time, some students recognize that they have trouble in certain types of learning situations. For example, some students of normal and even exceptional intelligence find it nearly impossible to copy information from the chalkboard. It can be reassuring for them to know that although their approach to learning differs from those of their peers, they can still learn well in an alternate setting. In such cases, recognition of the difficulty can actually enhance students' self-confidence by conveying the message that difficulty in learning does not mean that a student is not intelligent. Furthermore, when a learning support system offers an alternative setting, students can get back on track for successful learning, which itself boosts confidence.

Features of Learning Support

Learning support programs may be organized in many different ways. Although some approaches, particularly those related to the schedule, work better in elementary schools and others work better in high schools, certain features are common to every approach.

The Curriculum

In a school committed to the learning of all students, there is no reason to create a different curriculum for students with learning difficulties (with the obvious exception of ESL students). There is not a separate "LD" or "Title I" curriculum. It is through the curriculum, after all, that the state or district standards are translated into learning expectations. Students who need additional help learning the curriculum might benefit from a different instructional approach, different materials, more time, or smaller instructional steps. But the expectations *as embedded in the curriculum* should be the same for them all.

Student Eligibility

If student success is defined as "learning the established curriculum," then students become eligible for additional assistance when they need help learning that curriculum, as revealed through their poor performance on assessments aligned to that curriculum. This is very different from declaring students eligible if they score poorly on a standardized test; eligibility for learning support must be based on students' degree of success in the curriculum, rather than on some other criteria.

Because eligibility for learning support is based on student progress in the curriculum, it follows that the support system must permit shifts in the eligibility status of individuals. In other words, students should not be declared eligible for an entire school year and thus required to receive additional assistance whether they need it or not. All students may be designated as *potential* clients of learning support services; at any given time, only those who actually *need* the extra help will be receiving it.

Staffing for Learning Support

Learning support systems are usually staffed by teachers, sometimes assisted by instructional aides. As a general rule, a teacher with special-education credentials should coordinate the program.

Organization of Learning Support

Learning support systems can be organized in a variety of ways, a few which are discussed here.

Teachers or Instructional Aides Working in Classrooms

In the most fully integrated learning support model, support teachers or instructional aides work alongside regular teachers in the classroom, where they offer additional help to individuals or groups of students as requested by the "regular" teacher. Although this model does not permit additional instructional time for struggling students, it does allow for more intensive assistance.

A Learning Support Center

A learning support center is a central location within the school where the learning support staff helps students. These centers are open to students throughout the day and reflect what many teachers already know: namely, that some students require more time than others to master the same material.

Although learning support centers appear similar to traditional Title I or resource rooms, they have a very different philosophy. Students go to learning support centers to work on the school's regular curriculum, whereas many Title I and resource rooms establish a separate curriculum for their students. Of course, students may use different materials in the learning support center than they do in the regular classroom—cutting apples to understand fractions, for example, rather than listening to an abstract presentation—but the content is that of the school's regular curriculum.

Extended Day: Before or After School

An extended-day program is another way to provide students with additional instructional time. Such programs typically use the school library or learning support center before or after school, or both, and are usually staffed by teachers, instructional aides, or parent volunteers. An extended-day program is particularly beneficial to students whose homes are not quiet enough for study, or who need additional help available in order to successfully complete their homework.

Paying for Learning Support

Many educators have found that, through careful design, they can apply state and federal categorical funds for special education to pay for their learning support programs. This approach involves challenges, however: because large amounts of money may be involved, questions of learning support inevitably turn to the organization of programs that can be paid for by categorical funds, bearing in mind the regulations surrounding their use. These regulations center on the use of the funds only for supplemental purposes. School districts are not authorized to use federal or state categorical funds merely to supplant expenditures that they would have paid for otherwise from regular district funds. The models of learning support presented in this chapter, however—such as addi-

tional staff to assist in the classroom or the establishment of a learning support center—clearly qualify for categorical funding.

Single-Source Funding

The simplest way to use categorical funds for a learning support program is to designate different categories of funds for different types of needs—for example, Title I funds for reading and state remedial funds for math. As long as student eligibility can be flexibly defined, such an approach can work well. Of course, schools using this approach are obliged to keep all funds separate: a student who comes to a learning support center for help with math, and is subsequently found to need help with reading as well, may not be able to receive the latter. Similarly, although students qualifying for assistance under migrant funding may learn the same lessons as students supported by Title I money, they must be taught separately, because the teachers for each group of students are paid out of different types of funds.

Blended Funding

The most powerful approach to funding learning support programs is a blended strategy. Under such a system, students are not separated according to the root cause of their difficulties; regardless of whether they are behind their peers generally, their first language is not English, or their migrant status has disrupted their schooling, the fact is that they need help, which the learning support system exists to provide. Still, educators using a blended-funding approach must find a way to comply with the many regulations governing the use of categorical funds, and to track expenditures separately while simultaneously offering integrated services;

although the delivery of service can be merged, the funds cannot be. Records must therefore be meticulously maintained, but educators should never lose sight of the overall purpose of learning support: to provide timely assistance to students who have difficulty learning.

Summary

The learning support system provides the safety net for student success in the curriculum, and should permit no student to fall through the cracks of a school. The system benefits teachers as well, by giving them the help necessary to assist students who need it. Schools can pay for learning support in a variety of ways, the most effective of which is to use categorical funds that are already allocated to the school. As with many other aspects of the instructional program, flexibility is key to making learning support work; neither students nor teachers can perform at their best if they are locked into an immutable arrangement.

➤ ➤ ➤

	Poor	Basic	Exemplary
RUBRIC FOR LEARNING SUPPORT			
Attitude	Students who need additional help are regarded as inherently deficient or unlikely to succeed in the school's program. These attitudes result in lowered expectations by both students and teachers.	Attitudes toward students who receive additional help are mixed; while attempts are made to ensure that students are not stigmatized, these attempts are not wholly successful.	Additional support is available to students who need it; teachers do not intimate that the students are incapable of achieving at high levels. Expectations of both students and teachers towards student learning are undiminished.
Program Integration	The learning support program is run independently of the regular program, with lower curriculum expectations and different assessments.	Most aspects of the learning support program are integrated into the regular school program, but some differences are evident in the curriculum expectations.	The learning support program is fully integrated into the regular school program; students learn the same curriculum and are assessed using the same means.
Flexibility	The learning support system is rigidly implemented: students who need help languish while others who are less in need are served. Adjustments are not made in a timely fashion.	Some flexibility is built into the learning support program, and students are able to receive extra help in a fairly timely fashion. However, communication among all parties is less than ideal, and some needs go unmet.	The learning support program is highly flexible, enabling students who need extra assistance to receive it quickly. Adjustments are made as needed to ensure that all students receive the help they require for success.

13

Teaching

The capstone of any school improvement effort is the quality of teaching, which represents the single most important aspect of any school's program for ensuring student success. Various research studies, including those conducted by the National Commission on Teaching and America's Future, have concluded that external factors typically account for roughly half of the learning differences between groups of students, while internal factors account for the other half. A school's curriculum and grading and attendance policies should all be aligned with school goals, of course, but no improvement effort is complete without a serious investigation of the quality of teaching.

It is unfortunate that educators in the United States devote so much time and energy to articulating the curriculum and so little to perfecting their instructional techniques. Committees spend eons contemplating what books to include in the 9th grade English curriculum, for example, or whether subtraction with regrouping should be taught in the 2nd, 3rd, or 4th grade, but have relatively few discussions about what instructional strategies might best engage students with the novel selected for 9th grade English or help students to really understand subtraction with regrouping. Other nations apportion their resources somewhat differently: the Japanese, for instance, embrace the concept of "lesson study," in which teachers perfect a single lesson by observing and providing feedback to their colleagues as a form of mutual professional development to enhance student learning.

The Framework for Teaching

In my 1996 book, *Enhancing Professional Practice: A Framework for Teaching,* I provide teachers with an outline for successful instruction. In it, I divide the work of teaching into the following four domains.

Domain 1: Planning and Preparation

a. Demonstrating knowledge of content and pedagogy
b. Demonstrating knowledge of students
c. Selecting instructional goals
d. Demonstrating knowledge of resources
e. Designing coherent instruction
f. Assessing student learning

Domain 1 of my framework deals with a teacher's skill in designing instruction—organizing the content to be learned. This domain covers all aspects of instructional planning, beginning with a deep understanding of the content and pedagogy and an appreciation of the students and what they bring to the educational encounter. But understanding content is not sufficient; the material must be transformed through instructional design into sequences of activities and assignments that make it accessible to students. All aspects of the instructional design—learning activities, materials, teaching strategies—should be appropriate to both the students and the content. Similarly, assessment techniques must be appropriate, both in substance and in process, to the learning goals and to the students being assessed.

Domain 2: Classroom Environment

a. Creating an environment of respect and rapport
b. Establishing a culture for learning
c. Managing classroom procedures
d. Managing student behavior
e. Organizing physical space

The skills included in Domain 2 relate to the creation of a comfortable and respectful classroom environment that cultivates a culture for learning in which students feel safe taking risks. The atmosphere is businesslike, with noninstructional matters handled efficiently; student behavior is cooperative and nondisruptive, and the physical environment supports the stated instructional purposes.

Domain 3: Instruction

a. Communicating clearly and accurately
b. Using questioning and discussion techniques
c. Engaging students in learning
d. Providing feedback to students
e. Demonstrating flexibility and responsiveness

Domain 3 contains the skills that are at the heart of teaching: the actual engagement of students with the content. When noneducators describe what teachers do, they usually center on the skills in Domain 3. A teacher's level of proficiency in these skills affects how students experience the content, whether they grow to love it or hate it, and the extent to which they come to see school learning as important to their lives. Of course, teachers' instructional strategies should be supported by research on teaching and learning in their specific grades and fields; 3rd grade reading, 8th grade science, and high-school math all require different types of instruction.

Domain 4: Professional Responsibilities

a. Reflecting on teaching
b. Maintaining accurate records
c. Communicating with families
d. Contributing to the school and district
e. Growing and developing professionally
f. Showing professionalism

Domain 4 encompasses the roles teachers assume outside of the classroom. Students rarely observe the activities described here, and parents and the larger community observe them only intermittently. Still, maintaining accurate records, communicating with families, contributing to the school and district, and growing professionally all are critical to the preservation and enhancement of the teaching profession.

The framework for teaching is not designed to be highly original, but rather to reflect the "wisdom of practice" of educators. Although I developed it with the needs of new teachers in mind, to offer them a roadmap to the complex work of teaching, the framework has proved to be useful to all teachers, not only novices.

The Levels of Performance

Enhancing Professional Practice describes in narrative form each of the 22 components of the four domains, and defines four fundamental levels of performance: unsatisfactory, basic, proficient, and distinguished. Figure 13.1 illustrates the levels of performance for component 3b (using questioning and discussion techniques).

Although the types of skills described vary considerably from one component to another, underlying patterns of behavior are reflected in the different levels of the framework. Teachers who are performing at the "basic" level, for example, display common characteristics of practice in all aspects of their teaching.

At an unsatisfactory level of performance, teachers may actually be doing harm to their students—by creating instructional plans that are completely inappropriate to a given situation, for instance, or an environment that is physically dangerous to students or in which students are treated disrespectfully. Unsatisfactory instruction might be so poor that students cannot engage with the content, or are excluded from learning activities.

The basic level of performance is typical of student teachers and beginning teachers. These teachers, after all, are doing virtually everything for the first time; lessons rarely proceed according to plan. Activities can take more or less time than anticipated, and students might not understand the directions or might lack prerequisite knowledge. The learning experiences designed and implemented by teachers at this level tend to be a little rough around the edges; because beginning teachers rarely have a "plan B" to use when they encounter difficulty, they usually must just stumble through.

Teachers performing at the basic level are usually well prepared for their work; they know what the right thing to do is and they try to do it. However, their efforts tend to be inconsistent and not always completely successful for reasons that often are related to lack of experience. Working with a trained mentor and engaging in careful planning and structured reflection on practice can help such teachers to quickly become proficient. The proficient level of teacher performance is characterized by very professional and successful

	13.1 PERFORMANCE RUBRIC FOR COMPONENT 3B			
ELEMENT	**LEVEL OF PERFORMANCE**			
	Unsatisfactory	**Basic**	**Proficient**	**Distinguished**
Quality of Questions	Teacher's questions are virtually all of poor quality.	Teacher's questions are a combination of low and high quality. Only some invite a response.	Most of teacher's questions are of high quality. Adequate time is available for students to respond.	Teacher's questions are of uniformly high quality, with adequate time for students to respond. Students formulate many questions.
Discussion Techniques	Interaction between teacher and students is predominantly recitation style, with teacher mediating all questions and answers.	Teacher makes some attempt to engage students in a true discussion, with uneven results.	Classroom interaction represents true discussion, with teacher stepping to the side when appropriate.	Students assume considerable responsibility for the success of the discussion, initiating topics and making unsolicited contributions.
Student Participation	Only a few students participate in the discussion.	Teacher attempts to engage all students in the discussion, but with only limited success.	Teacher successfully engages all students in the discussion.	Students themselves ensure that all voices are heard in the discussion.

teaching; most experienced teachers perform at this level. These teachers know their content and their students, and are able to design learning experiences that are aligned to content standards and engaging to students. They possess an instructional repertoire and know when to use which strategies. Teachers performing at the proficient level know what they are about; they have techniques to fall back on and are rarely taken by surprise. They are professional educators.

The distinguished level is reserved for accomplished teachers who have created environments that are truly communities of learners. In these classrooms, the students themselves have assumed considerable responsibility; it is their classroom too, and they help to make it work. Instruction at the distinguished level can look deceptively easy. To the untrained eye, such a class looks like magic—all involved know what to do, go about their business without rancor, spend their time productively, and so on.

Some find it helpful to think metaphorically about the levels of performance. If we apply a swimming analogy, then teachers performing at the unsatisfactory level are drowning, at the basic level they're doing the dog paddle, at the proficient level they've mastered the backstroke and sidestroke, and at the distinguished level they are competitive swimmers who devote considerable time and energy to training and improving performance. They may also be serving as swimming coaches to less proficient swimmers.

We should always bear in mind that the levels in the framework refer to levels of *teaching performance,* not of *teachers.* Teaching itself is highly variable and dependent on context; for example, a teacher is more likely to demonstrate high-level performance—i.e., proficient or distinguished—in May than in September. Similarly, teachers who are reassigned to unfamiliar subjects or grade levels will find their performance to be weaker than usual, at least at the beginning, in the new setting. Such teachers, in fact, are confronted with many of the same challenges that a novice teacher would face: a new curriculum, unfamiliar students, and an inadequate repertoire of instructional strategies appropriate to the new assignment. In addition, some students present teachers with tremendous instructional challenges; for example, it may take even an experienced teacher most of a year to create a community of learners with a group of students who are angry and alienated from school.

The Uses of Assessment

Teachers in schools with an uncompromising commitment to student learning use assessment strategies extensively; after all, assessments provide evidence of success (or lack thereof) for both students and teachers.

External Assessments

There are many different types of external assessments, including advanced placement exams, state assessments, and end-of-course tests. External assessments are typically high-stakes, although they do not have to be. Whatever the source and regardless of their uses, external assessments can help clarify student expectations and encourage a sense of partnership between teachers and students.

The existence of external assessments serves to define the learning expectations for a course, grade level, or level of schooling and therefore serve as operational definitions of the curriculum: they define what students should know and be able to do as a result of their learning. Such clarity is useful for both students and teachers.

If assessments are to clarify expectations, they should be made public; their value is diminished if their contents are secret. Of course, the contents of a high-stakes test cannot be disclosed in their entirety, lest students be able to formulate correct answers beforehand. However, a *version* of the test can be disclosed, clearly identified as equivalent to but different from the test that will "count." Such disclosed tests help teachers to organize their instruction and students to structure their learning, and remove the sense of mystery and arbitrariness that tends to accompany high-stakes assessment.

The very existence of external tests can transform the relationship between students and teachers. All teachers want their students to do well, and some base their reputations on their students' success on, say, advanced placement tests. Because the tests are external, students get the sense that the teacher's job is to work with them to do as well as possible; rather than playing the role of judge with students—as they do when they themselves develop the tests—the teachers become more like co-conspirators. The teacher and students are thus more inclined to work together to prepare for the assessments. Although this phenomenon is more pronounced in high schools than in elementary schools, it can be in evidence everywhere.

Formative Assessment and Feedback on Learning

Educators who want to ensure student learning must make use of formative assessment and feedback. Formative assessments are standards-based but have as their sole purpose student learning; because there are no immediate consequences for poor performances, formative tests are not high-stakes. The assessment and the feedback that accompany formative tests are designed only to support learning.

Curriculum and Instructional Alignment

Some teachers are uncomfortable with the concept of aligning instruction with the curriculum. Because assessments are aligned to the curriculum, these teachers believe that to do the same with instruction would be "teaching to the test."

Teaching to the Test

Educators who "teach to the test" know the items that will be on the test and fashion their instruction to match. (In many cases, the teachers may have actually created the test.) They may know, for example, that on the 7th grade science test students will be asked to identify the correct

definition for "buoyancy" from a selection of statements, and thus have their students memorize the definition so they could do well on the test. By proceeding in this manner, teachers are violating the spirit of the assessment: to determine whether students *understand* a main concept of the course, for example buoyancy, and how it relates to sinking and floating and other concepts, such as density. Assessments can test only a small portion of the knowledge that educators want students to learn; tests represent only a sample of important knowledge and skill. If teachers restrict their instruction to only that which they know for certain will be on the test, then they are denying their students important learning experiences. Teaching to the test, then, cannot be justified.

Teaching to the Curriculum

On the other hand, it is perfectly legitimate for teachers to "teach to the curriculum." In fact, that is what they *should* do, since the curriculum is aligned to state or district content standards. When assessments are also aligned to these standards, some teachers will consider teaching to the curriculum to be the same as teaching to the test. They are not the same, however: when teachers teach to the curriculum, they are teaching in such a manner that *students learn the curriculum content*. If the curriculum is stated in terms of conceptual understanding and performance rather than rote memorization alone, students are likely to have a rich educational experience. As long as students understand the important concepts they are taught in class, they will be able to do well on assessments.

Teachers should never feel that it is unethical to teach to the curriculum; on the contrary, it is unethical *not* to. A teacher's job is to prepare students for challenges that will come their way, including being able to demonstrate skill on state, district, and school assessments. If assessments are aligned to the curriculum, instruction should be as well; only then can students be successful.

Summary

Teaching, of course, is at the heart of the school's instructional program and makes the largest single contribution to student learning. Although teaching is primarily the responsibility of individual teachers, teamwork and joint planning can enhance its effectiveness. The complex work of teaching is captured in the framework for teaching summarized in this chapter. When this framework is used in a school deeply committed to the success of all students and in combination with other systems of organization, highly positive results can be expected.

➤ ➤ ➤

		RUBRIC FOR TEACHING	
	Poor	**Basic**	**Exemplary**
Domain 1: Planning and Preparation	Teacher demonstrates little knowledge of content, pedagogy, and students. Instructional goals, resources and materials, and instructional design are loosely connected, ineffective, or poorly adapted to the needs of individual students.	Teacher demonstrates adequate knowledge of content, pedagogy, and students. Instructional goals, resources and materials, and instructional design are all connected and somewhat adapted to the needs of individual students.	Teacher demonstrates in-depth knowledge of content, pedagogy, and students. Instructional goals, resources and materials, and instructional design are tightly connected and highly effective and are well adapted to the needs of individual students.
Domain 2: The Classroom Environment	Interactions between students and between the teacher and students are inappropriate or disrespectful. Classroom procedures and management of student behavior are vaguely defined or ineffective, contributing to a poor learning environment. Physical space is poorly or unsafely organized.	Interactions between students and between the teacher and students are respectful. Classroom procedures are clear, and student behavior is managed with little or no loss of instructional time. Physical space is adequately organized to support learning.	Interactions between students and between the teacher and students are appropriate and respectful, with high expectations for learning. Classroom procedures are seamless and establish a challenging and dynamic environment for learning. Physical space is skillfully and safely organized to support learning. Students themselves make a substantive contribution to the smooth functioning of the classroom.
Domain 3: Instruction	Students are uninvolved or only partially engaged in learning as a result of poor communication, low-level questions, little student participation in discussion, little or no feedback on learning, and the teacher's rigid adherence to an instructional plan despite evidence that it should be modified.	Students are engaged in learning as a result of clear communication, appropriate instructional strategies, and productive use of feedback. The teacher demonstrates flexibility when contributing to the success of the lesson and of each student.	All students are highly engaged in learning, and make material contributions to the success of the class by asking questions and participating in discussions, getting actively involved in learning activities, and using feedback in their learning. The teacher ensures the success of every student by creating a high-level learning environment; providing timely, high-quality feedback; and continuously searching for approaches that meet student needs.
Domain 4: Professional Responsibilities	Teacher maintains inaccurate or incomplete records, communicates irregularly or ineffectively with families, and does not adequately support the school or district. Professional development is misinformed or trivial. Reflection on teaching is nonexistent or tangential.	Teacher demonstrates a sense of professionalism by reflecting on instruction, maintaining accurate records, communicating frequently with families, actively participating in school and district events, and engaging in activities for professional development.	Teacher's sense of professionalism is highly developed, reflecting perceptive use of reflection, effective record keeping and communication with families, and leadership roles in both school and district projects and professional development activities.

	Poor	Basic	Exemplary
RUBRIC FOR TEACHING (CONTINUED)			
Use of Student Assessment	Teachers only use student assessment data for assigning grades to students, and provide little or no feedback to students on their learning.	Teachers attempt to use student assessment data for more than student grading, with uneven results. They offer limited feedback to students and use the data only intermittently to improve their practice.	Teachers use student assessment data to provide specific and timely feedback to students, reflect on their own practice, monitor progress towards content standards, and contribute to student grades.

Part 3:

Implementing the Framework

Chapter 14 suggests to readers how they might use the concepts presented in this book to make good on the promise of the framework presented in Part 2—namely, to ensure that all students are learning. Putting the framework into practice is not a simple process; a number of separate items must be attended to, and every school already has systems in place, some of which may meet the performance standards recommended in this book. Educators may therefore use Part 3 as a means of assessing the school program as a whole.

14

Action Planning

School improvement does not happen by itself. Serious school improvement, along the lines described in this book, does not consist of merely fiddling around the edges of the school's organization, implementing a single new program, or establishing a partnership with a business in the community; rather, the process should be comprehensive and should encompass everything done in the school. Research confirms what educators know well from their own experience: that visionary leadership makes an extraordinary difference in any complex undertaking. A comprehensive project of school improvement requires clarity of vision, breadth of view, and a determination to overcome inevitable obstacles that permits others to participate with confidence. Many teachers are weary of constant change, and are not convinced that the latest new program will be any improvement over the old way of doing things. Because teachers recognize that they will likely still be teaching at the same school long after the principal has left, they can easily adopt an attitude of "this too shall pass."

Leaders of serious school improvement efforts face the challenge of marshalling the energy and expertise of their staff in the service of the project. A leader's skills extend far beyond running meetings efficiently; clarifying a vision for school improvement, helping staff members to understand how their daily work supports (or possibly undermines) the vision, and serving as an advocate for both students and staff are all critical for success. It is essential that teachers and support staff regard their actions in light of the core mission of the school: ensuring student success.

Leadership does not reside solely with administrators; in many schools, team leaders or department chairs also serve as educational leaders. However, administrators must also develop and exercise strong leadership. The very positions of principal and assistant principal include within their job descriptions the exercise of leadership within the school; without this leadership, no school improvement effort can succeed. The activities described in this chapter are assumed to be under the direction of a visionary administrative leader who sees the big picture as well as the details and who can help a school's staff maintain forward momentum.

Developing Consensus on the Foundation

The foundation of any school program is predicated on a clear grasp of the school's goals, belief structure, and research base. Any school improvement effort should begin with consensus in those areas.

Establishing Consensus on "What We Want"

It is essential for a school community to be exceedingly clear about its broad goals, which should encompass student learning, the professional culture, and the school's relationship with its larger community. Some goals, particularly those related to student achievement, will later be articulated in the school's curriculum; one reasonable aim, therefore, might be for all students to master the curriculum. Other goals might include

the establishment of a professional culture of collaborative inquiry, a positive environment for students and their families, and links with the broader community.

Many schools have experience developing mission statements, and thus will have given thought to these goals. Such statements typically reflect a philosophy, and include such broad objectives as "helping each student reach his or her potential" or "meeting the intellectual, social, and physical needs of all students." Some mission statements may overlap with statements of "what we want." Unlike the former, however, the latter must be written in a manner that provides specific direction. A set of statements about "what we want" might look something like this:

> ➤ High-level learning for all students (including but not restricted to achievement of state or district content standards)
> ➤ A positive culture for students
> ➤ A culture of professional inquiry for teachers
> ➤ The school as a center for learning in the community

In general, fewer goals are better than more; as will be seen later in this chapter, just a few significant goals can generate many demands for data collection and analysis. In addition, each broad goal includes a number of sub-goals, each of which should be examined and analyzed individually.

Establishing Consensus on "What We Believe"

School practices rest on assumptions that are deeply held but frequently unexamined by both educators and the community, virtually ensuring that schools are resistant to meaningful change. Any process of school improvement must include systematic attention to the beliefs that influence action, policies, and practices in the school. This process is not easy, and suggests an important role for leadership. Educators must connect beliefs to actions and point out when certain actions are incompatible with stated beliefs. The examination of beliefs is challenging and may be uncomfortable, since the beliefs may stand in contrast sharply with *facts*. It is easy to adopt noble-sounding but essentially superficial belief statements, such as the ubiquitous "all children can learn." Such a statement, when combined with the extensive evidence that not all students are in fact learning well, cries out for an explanation. If all children can learn, but only a small percentage has passed the state's test of its content standards, why is this? If a school also adopts the belief that "schools control the conditions of success," then its educators can't let themselves off the hook for poor student performance.

These considerations confront educators with another challenge: namely, their own professional confidence. If a school adopts the belief that all students can achieve at high levels if they apply themselves and commit to learning, the teachers must believe that they can make good on the promise; adults in a school must believe that—through their work in the classroom and with the programs, policies, and procedures they establish in the school—they can ensure successful learning by all students.

Unfortunately, not all educators have this much confidence in their own abilities; perhaps their professional preparation was weak, or they are not aware of new developments in instruc-

tional approaches, or maybe they lack sufficient time to prepare lessons that ensure student engagement and learning. Whatever the case, many educators fear that they don't have what it takes to guarantee student success, and it becomes easier for them to blame anything—students, parents, the schedule, the system—but themselves for the poor performance of their students. Lacking confidence in their own abilities, many educators succumb to the prevailing social attitude that school success is highly correlated with the socioeconomic status of students' families and that there is not a lot they can do to overcome this fact.

The process used to establish a school's beliefs must respect the highly personal nature of these types of beliefs and their tight connection to results. Those leading the process of establishing beliefs for a school must ensure that everyone involved is treated with respect, and that individuals are not cornered into defending beliefs that might undermine the school's goals: for example, a teacher who defends the bell curve on the grounds that it maintains high standards should not be attacked for his views. But if the school culture is such that the teacher cannot admit to his beliefs, the beliefs will simply go "underground," continuing to influence his practice, but hidden from public view. The professional culture must be one of respect and mutual exploration; individuals must feel safe stating their views. They must also be provided time and support to change them.

Establishing Consensus on "What We Know"

Educators in any school trying to improve student learning must stay abreast of current research in education, psychology, organizational development, and so on. This is a tall order, made more challenging by the following factors:

➤ **The faddish nature of education.**
Education is a profession prone to fads: there is always a reform practice *du jour* that will be superseded by tomorrow's trend, and woe betide the educator who implements yesterday's craze today. Cooperative learning may be all the rage one day, only to be replaced in the professional consciousness by multiple intelligences. It is as though there can be only one "truth" at a time; attending to more than one aspect of practice appears to be the educational equivalent of walking and chewing gum simultaneously.

➤ **Little time available for staying current.**
Most educators are extremely busy people, so time is often the scarcest resource of all. Teachers and administrators have very little time to devote to scholarly pursuits; just staying current in their respective fields is enough of a challenge for many. Not only do educators need to stay abreast of current developments in educational research—they must also understand the impact of research on daily operations. Therefore, educators must pay attention to findings related to learning in general, such as those that deal with class size, grouping practices, and motivation.

Schools must adopt a coherent approach to keeping current with research. One possibility is as follows:

➤ To satisfy district or state requirements for professional development, teachers within a school are assigned a professional journal (e.g., *Educational Leadership, Phi Delta Kappan, Learning K-8, Instructor,* journals devoted to individual disciplines).

➤ The teachers each assume responsibility for monitoring the articles in their respective journals and determining how the articles' findings relate to the school's program.

➤ The teachers summarize the articles that they think have something to offer the rest of the faculty—perhaps as part of faculty, grade-level, or departmental meetings. If appropriate, they distribute copies of articles to colleagues.

Because these activities satisfy requirements for professional development, they may be undertaken by teachers without the sense that they are yet another burden added to their already overloaded jobs.

Reviewing and Revising Policies and Practices for Consistency with Research Base, Beliefs, and Goals

It is not unusual for a school to inherit policies and practices that are inconsistent with its own stated beliefs and goals or disavowed by recent research. Many schools operate without a clearly defined curriculum, approach to scheduling, or system of learning support. Such practices can persist without anyone really noticing that they are actually undermining the school's stated goals with respect to student learning. Unless these practices are changed, the desired results will never be achieved.

School Organization, Policies Regarding Students and Staff, and Linkages Beyond the School

Student attendance and homework policies at a school may be incompatible with a success orientation, or the school's procedures for teacher evaluation or professional development may not contribute to a culture of respect and professional inquiry. And a school's master schedule may make it more difficult to implement the type of instruction that teachers believe would promote higher levels of student learning. Of course, revising these systems is not a small undertaking; the procedures have usually been in place for a long time and are familiar to the students and staff. Even if educators are inclined to revise certain policies and practices, there is a limit to the number of major initiatives that a school's staff can manage simultaneously; many schools encounter "reform fatigue" when they embark on multiple projects at the same time or in rapid succession. On the other hand, dysfunctional practices should not be permitted to remain intact, particularly if they are actually working at cross-purposes to the school's major goals.

There is no easy solution to this difficulty, which is chiefly a resource problem: Where should staff spend its time and energy? Which projects are most critical, and which can wait? Clearly, planning is essential. As deficiencies are noted, it is important that a plan enabling educators to address the most serious concerns first, followed by others of lower priority, be implemented.

Program Organization

Daily instruction is directly supported by, and cannot be wholly successful without, attending to the different aspects of the school program's organization. Teachers cannot teach well without a clear curriculum aligned to the state or district content standards, well-designed assessments, clear and flexible procedures for assigning students and teachers, and a learning support plan. Without these systems in place, teachers' efforts are seriously compromised; they simply cannot accomplish their best work.

Of course, if a school does not have a coherent curriculum or aligned assessments in place, it is not going to acquire them overnight. Such projects require considerable effort and time yet are critical for successful teaching and learning. If found to require attention, then, such matters should be addressed with all deliberate speed.

Implementing a Process of Continuous Improvement

The quality movement has had an enormous impact on many companies in the private sector: by paying systematic attention to the details of their operations, companies have seen increased productivity, efficiency, and customer satisfaction. Employees at companies that invest in quality initiatives typically experience a considerable degree of job satisfaction as a result of their direct participation in (and sense of responsibility for) the company. If the company manufactures products, there are fewer defects and returns and less waste. If the company sells insurance, records are well kept, customer satisfaction is high, and profits are healthy. And in all cases, employee morale is high, deriving from a sense of satisfaction that comes from a job well done.

Although few schools have made a formal commitment to a quality program, all can implement many aspects of such an approach. School improvement requires educators to define and identify indicators of that success; it also involves an unflinching examination of evidence (typically through data collection and analysis) and an uncompromising commitment to action.

Indicators of Success

For each of a school's goals, educators must determine indicators of success, the school's current degree of attainment, and reasonable targets for improvement. In order to do this, they must pay particular attention to how the goals are assessed. Clearly, the evidence of different types of goals must be appropriate to each type. And student test scores on standardized tests are only one among many sources of evidence; although they are important pieces of information, they fail to provide anything like a comprehensive answer to the question of "how are we doing." As practitioners recognize the power of becoming data-driven, they must take seriously the matter of determining what serve as indicators of success for all their important goals. Figure 14.1 is intended to provide educators with guidance for local thinking and decision making about data collection and analysis, but is not an ironclad prescription for program evaluation.

The sources of evidence named in this chart are fairly extensive, and may include more data than educators in many schools are able to collect. Of course, some sources can serve as evidence for multiple goals: for example, a single student survey could be designed to provide information on students' views about the school's atmosphere of safety, its rewards for hard work, and their opportunities for leadership within the school.

Collection and Analysis of Baseline Data

Few schools would ever collect and analyze all the data suggested in Figure 14.1; choices must be made and priorities set according to the time and energy available. Still, systematic planning is essential, and individual staff assignments for data collection must be able to be incorporated into normal school routines. In addition, educators should consider the effect of using data gathering and analysis for promoting a professional culture. When teachers disaggregate their end-of-course assessment results, for example, they gain insight into their teaching that is not available by any other means. Similarly, a group of teachers can identify areas of their school's curriculum needing improvement by analyzing the state's assessment of content standards.

It is important for all teachers to be involved in data collection and analysis, as all educators should become more data-driven and more focused on results. Such an arrangement promotes a spirit of problem solving and collaboration, particularly when improving school performance is regarded (as it should be) as a team effort. Because of the time required for data collection and analysis, both activities must be carefully planned. In addition, different teachers should have different assignments: some could be responsible for designing and administering student surveys, for example, whereas others could be in charge of gathering information related to student attendance or analyzing course enrollments by student ethnicity.

	14.1 Possible Data Sources for Different Goal Areas		
Goal	**Description**	**Possible Indicators**	**Sources of Evidence**
High Level Learning for All Students			
All students have access to a rigorous curriculum	Students are taught for *understanding*, in a challenging curriculum, rather than only rote repetition.	➤ Curriculum outcomes reflect rigorous learning. ➤ Assignments and activities require students to develop and demonstrate understanding. ➤ Classroom teaching engages students in higher-order thinking and problem solving. ➤ Course offerings are challenging and are appropriate to level.	➤ Curriculum analysis ➤ Random sampling of assignments and student work ➤ Classroom observations ➤ AP course offerings or equivalent
Students learn at high levels	Virtually all students master the basic (but rigorous) curriculum.	➤ High passing rates on state assessments. ➤ High grades on school-based assessments and end-of-course exams.	➤ State assessment data ➤ School grades
All students succeed at high levels	High averages do not conceal large differences in achievement between different subgroups of students.	➤ Students from all groups enrolled in high-level courses and skill groups. ➤ State assessment results show high levels of performance of all groups of students. ➤ School-based assessments show high levels of performance of all groups of students.	➤ Course and ability groups analyzed by sub-group ➤ State test results disaggregated by sub-group ➤ School-based assessments disaggregated by sub-group ➤ Student dropout rates
A rich and varied school program	The school program develops not only cognitive skills, but also interpersonal skills, dispositions, aesthetics, athletics, and responsibility.	➤ Curriculum guides articulate varied outcomes. ➤ The school program includes opportunities for students in the visual and performing arts, and athletics, as well as in academic subjects. ➤ Classroom instruction includes, where appropriate, varied types of goals. ➤ Feedback to students and comments to parents include information on varied goals.	➤ Curriculum analysis ➤ Analysis of program offerings ➤ Classroom observation ➤ Classroom observation, samples of student work with feedback, and reports to parents

	14.1 POSSIBLE DATA SOURCES FOR DIFFERENT GOAL AREAS (CONTINUED)		
Goal	**Description**	**Possible Indicators**	**Sources of Evidence**
A Positive Culture for Students			
Environment physically safe and attractive	The physical environment is free of hazards such as peeling paint, falling ceilings, violent weapons, and nonfunctioning water fountains and restrooms. In addition, equipment and supplies are adequate, student work is displayed, and the environment conveys a focus on learning.	➤ Absence of physical hazards. ➤ Adequate equipment and supplies. ➤ Classroom furniture arranged to be conducive to learning. ➤ Classrooms and public areas honor student learning.	➤ Observation throughout the school, absence of concern by students, staff and parents ➤ Classroom observation, absence of concern by staff and parents
Environment emotionally safe	The school environment is a safe place for students, tolerant of diversity of appearance and views.	➤ Students are not belittled by teachers or staff. ➤ Students not subjected to ridicule or bullying by other students. ➤ Students feel respected.	➤ Phone calls from parents ➤ Incident reports from playground ➤ Observation of interactions ➤ Student surveys ➤ Student focus groups
Hard work valued and rewarded	Student perseverance, effort, and application are cultivated and rewarded.	➤ Teachers promote student effort in the classroom. ➤ Grading system reflects effort as well as achievement. ➤ Students believe that hard work is important.	➤ Classroom observation ➤ Feedback to students in the classroom and on student work ➤ Report cards ➤ Student surveys ➤ Student focus groups
School culture recognizes student excellence in many arenas	Student contributions and achievements (progress as well as absolute levels) in scholarship, the arts, athletics, etc., receive recognition.	➤ Awards, displays of student work, and public recognition of student achievement includes virtually all students.	➤ Analysis of recognition patterns
Students have multiple opportunities for success	Initial difficulty in learning is not perceived, by students or teachers, to indicate that success is not possible.	➤ Classroom interactions encourage multiple attempts to learn content (neither students nor teachers "give up"). ➤ Support systems are available to provide additional assistance as needed. ➤ The grading system does not discourage multiple attempts.	➤ Classroom observation ➤ Analysis of support systems (Title I, LEP, etc.) ➤ Analysis of grading systems used

	14.1 POSSIBLE DATA SOURCES FOR DIFFERENT GOAL AREAS (CONTINUED)		
Goal	**Description**	**Possible Indicators**	**Sources of Evidence**
Students have multiple opportunities for initiative, responsibility, and leadership	Students are viewed not only as "clients" of the school, but also as contributing partners to its culture; they deliberate on issues that affect them and serve in roles such as office and laboratory aides, tutors to younger students, etc.	➤ High percentages of students are involved in leadership roles; these roles are not dominated by a few students. ➤ Students believe that they can make a positive contribution to the school.	➤ Analysis of participation lists for various activities and responsibilities ➤ Student surveys ➤ Student focus groups
A Culture of Professional Inquiry for Teachers			
All teachers engaged in high-quality professional learning	Professional development is self-directed, is focused on enhanced student learning, is job-embedded and collaborative, and is continuous and ongoing.	➤ Time is available for teachers to engage in important professional inquiry. ➤ The professional culture expects all teachers to participate and supports collaboration and professional inquiry. ➤ Professional activities satisfy state requirements for relicensing.	➤ School schedule ➤ Teacher survey ➤ Analysis of re-licensing records
Professional inquiry is recognized and rewarded	There are opportunities for teachers to share and celebrate their investigations and findings.	➤ Time is available in staff meetings for professional sharing and celebration. ➤ Results of professional work are distributed to teachers in other schools. ➤ Teachers are encouraged to attend professional conferences, either as participants or presenters.	➤ Faculty meeting agendas ➤ Newsletters, other communications ➤ Memos to staff, teacher records of participation, staff survey

14.1 POSSIBLE DATA SOURCES FOR DIFFERENT GOAL AREAS (CONTINUED)			
Goal	**Description**	**Possible Indicators**	**Sources of Evidence**
The School as a Center for Learning in the Community			
Use of school facilities by community groups	Community education and health services programs are available in public school buildings.	➤ School buildings are rarely empty. ➤ School personnel coordinates efforts with representatives from other groups that use the school facilities.	➤ Schedule of use ➤ Records of arrangements made for supplies, custodial services, supplies, etc.
Public perception of accessibility	Members of the public regard school facilities as resources for them.	➤ Attendance at community-sponsored activities is large and growing.	➤ Attendance records ➤ Community Surveys
Communication with parents, community and business leaders	Parents, community, and business leaders are familiar with the school's programs.	➤ Parent newsletters ➤ Presentations to community and business groups	➤ Parent surveys ➤ Community surveys
Partnerships with businesses and community agencies	The school establishes partnerships with local agencies and businesses.	➤ Community agency and business personnel visit the schools ➤ Students and teachers participate in learning activities in businesses and community agencies	➤ Records of visits from community agencies and businesses ➤ Records of involvement of teachers and students in community agencies and businesses

Establishing S.M.A.R.T. Objectives

Once school personnel have acquired comprehensive baseline data, they can use it to establish objectives for improvement. For example, if the data analysis reveals that 53 percent of the school's algebra students achieved a grade last year of *A* or *B* on the end-of-course exam (reflecting mastery of a given portion of the curriculum), teachers must establish a reasonable objective for the current year: would it be 60 percent or 65 percent?

Little else motivates people as well as do clear, worthwhile, and attainable objectives. They provide a focus for energy and action, and achieving them offers tremendous satisfaction to educators.

Trivial goals invite trivial effort, and educators who attain them feel that they have not accomplished much. Worthwhile goals reflecting broad aspirations, on the other hand, encourage serious effort and yield great satisfaction when achieved.

Good objectives translate broad, long-term goals into prescriptions for action. In addition to being short-term, they are specific, measurable, attainable, relevant, and time-bound—in other words, S.M.A.R.T.:

➤ **Specific.** Good objectives are not vague or general. Although we may want our students to behave more respectfully, a specific objective would not state, "students will be more respected by their peers"; instead, it might specify that bullying should decrease by, say, 50 percent.

➤ **Measurable.** Good objectives are measurable. Let's say that a school wants its female students to have a greater sense of confidence in math and science. A worthy goal! But how would it be measured? Confident students are more likely to enroll in advanced courses, and will probably earn better grades in them. Because proxy measures for confidence will have to be used, it makes sense to express the objective in a directly measurable form, such as "20 percent greater female participation and achievement in advanced mathematics and science courses."

➤ **Attainable.** Good objectives are not so far from current performance levels that they cannot be achieved, but they still present a challenge. Appropriate goals represent a manageable stretch from present levels, and serve to inspire rather than discourage effort. Achieving even a small goal can motivate people to pursue the next ones.

In addition, objectives that are challenging yet attainable can contribute enormously to a faculty's sense of community and common purpose; it is in achieving their goals, after all, that members of a school faculty come together as a team. Good teamwork is highly energizing and made meaningful by the common pursuit of important goals.

➤ **Relevant.** Good objectives are relevant to the purpose of the school. It would be possible to formulate objectives that meet all the other criteria but that aren't really relevant to the school's broader purposes; however, worthy goals should concern themselves with the school's core mission, not with tangential but easily measured matters. For example, a school team might establish as an objective that "86 percent of students bring their lunch to school." This is specific, and measurable, but who cares? What is the connection, if any, between students bringing their lunch to school and the attainment of important school goals?

➤ **Time-bound.** Lastly, good objectives have specific deadlines. They are not to be achieved "some time in the future," but rather "by May of next year," or some such date. A time limit allows people to focus their energies by setting a cut-off date. Deadlines are closely related to the issue of attainability, of course: certain objectives might be attainable next year, but not this year.

Planning and Implementing Actions to Achieve the Objectives

Action plans will reflect the same focus whether the established objectives are schoolwide or related to small groups of students. For example, if a survey reveals that students don't believe they have the opportunities to play leadership roles in the school, the issue of student leadership would probably be addressed at least initially as a matter for schoolwide decision making and action.

Clearly, the planning guidelines described in this chapter can be used by any school or even by individual teachers. Many states and districts mandate planning activities for their schools, and the plans that would emerge from the process discussed here would certainly meet their requirements.

Monitoring Indicators of Goal Achievement

Some might think of the collection and analysis of baseline data as a one-shot effort, particularly if it represents a departure from past practice. It may have required educators to plan and prioritize as well as to allocate resources beyond what had previously been dedicated to the purpose. It can only be hoped that such efforts, once expended, will have been seen to be valuable.

But the collection and analysis of data is not a one-shot affair; it must be a *habit*. Data regarding student achievement, attendance, and dropout rates must continue to be collected, disaggregated, and analyzed on a regular basis. Likewise, student, parent, and teacher attitudes; the condition of the physical plant; and activities with local businesses, colleges and universities, and community agencies must continue to be monitored.

Because most jobs require their employees to know how to collect and analyze data and communicate the results, there is an important role here for students. Naturally, students of different ages will contribute differently to the effort, but all can play a part, whether by suggesting questions for the student survey, comparing this year's data to last year's, or determining the best approach—graph, table, raw numbers—to communicate the data analysis results to the entire school community.

Recognizing and Celebrating Progress

This step is frequently skipped, and it should not be! By the time they have implemented an ambitious school improvement effort, many educators are too drained to step back and celebrate their efforts. They should, however, do so: recognition and celebration of progress is a high-profile activity that is most successful when broadly shared; students, parents, community, and all staff should be involved in meaningful ways. Members of the support staff should be recognized for their contributions to the life of the school. The celebration of progress should be a validation of the school's program and of its school improvement efforts, communicating to the entire community what the school is about, what it stands for, and what is important.

Summary

When educators "put it all together" to improve their schools for enhanced student learning and success, they enjoy the greatest exhilaration that the profession can offer: bringing their entire expertise to bear on providing a first-rate education to all children. What could be more exciting than that? The satisfaction of making a difference in the lives of young people, of seeing them become successful, is what keeps educators in this demanding and at times trying profession.

➤ ➤ ➤

Bibliography

Achilles, C. M. (1997, October). Small classes, big possibilities. *School Administrator,* 6–15.

Archibold, R. C. (2001, January 14). What kind of education is adequate? It depends. *New York Times,* p. A33.

Alleman, J. E., & Brophy, J. (2000). On the menu: the growth of self-efficacy. *Social Studies and the Young Learner, 12*(3), 15–19.

Anderson, J. (1994, March). Alternative approaches to organizing the school day and year. *School Administrator,* 8–11.

Anderson, L., Everston, C., & Brophy, J. (1979). An experimental study of effective teaching in 1st-grade reading groups. *Elementary School Journal, 79,* 193–223.

Atkinson, J. (1975). Motivational determinants of risk-taking behaviour. *Psychological Review, 64,* 359–372.

Balkcom, S. (1992, June). Cooperative learning. *Education Research Consumer Guide,* 1.

Barth, R. (1990). *Improving schools from within.* San Francisco, CA: Jossey-Bass.

Bates, J. T. (1993). Portrait of a successful rural alternative school. *Rural Educator, 14*(3), 20–24.

Battistich, V., Solomon, D., & Delucchi, K. (1993). Interaction processes and student outcomes in cooperative learning groups. *Elementary School Journal, 94*(1), 19–32.

Blase, J., & Blase, J. (1997). *The fire is back: Principals sharing school governance.* Thousand Oaks, CA: Corwin Press.

Brophy, J. (1981). Teacher praise: A functional analysis. *Review of Educational Research, 51*(1), 20–25.

Brophy, J. (1986). Teacher influences on student achievement. *American Psychologist, 41*(10), 1069–1077.

Brophy, J., & Good, T. (1986). Research linking teacher behavior to student achievement: Potential implications for instruction. In M. Wittrock (Ed.), *Handbook of Research on Teaching* (pp. 328–375). New York: Macmillan.

Burke, A. M. (1987). *Making a big school smaller: The school-within-a-school arrangement for middle-level schools.* Orting, WA: Publisher. (ERIC Document Reproduction Service No. ED 303 890)

Canady, R. L., & Rettig, M. D. (1995). *Block scheduling: A catalyst for change in high schools.* Princeton, NJ: Eye on Education.

Canady, R. L., & Rettig, M. D. (2000). Block scheduling: What have we learned? In W. G. Wraga & P. S. Hlebowitsh (Eds.), *Research review for school leaders* (355–382). Mahwah, NJ: Erlbaum Publishers.

Canady, R. L., & Rettig, M. D. (2001). Block scheduling: The key to quality learning time. *Principal, 80*(3), 30–34.

Cain, K. M., & Dweck, C. (1995). The relation between motivational patterns and achievement cognitions through the elementary school years. *Merrill Palmer Quarterly, 41,* 25–52.

Carpenter, W. A. (2000). Ten years of silver bullets dissenting thoughts on educational reform. *Phi Delta Kappan, 81*(5), 383–389.

Cawelti, G. (1993, Summer). Restructuring large high schools to personalize learning for all. *ERS Spectrum, 11*(3), 17–21.

Cohen, D. K., & Hill, H. C. (1998, January). State policy and classroom performance. *CPRE Policy Briefs.*

Cohen, D. K., Raudenbush, S. W., & Loewenberg-Ball, D. (2000, December). *Resources, instruction, and research: A CTP working paper.* Seattle: Center for the Study of Teaching and Policy, University of Washington.

Coleman, J. (1961). *Slums and suburbs: A commentary on schools in metropolitan areas.* New York: McGraw-Hill.

Coleman, J. (1966). *Equality of educational opportunity survey.* Washington, DC: U.S. Government Printing Office.

Coleman, J., Schneider, B., Plank, S., Schiller, K. S., Shouse, R., Wang, H., & Lee, S. (1997). *Redesigning American education.* Boulder, CO: Westview Press.

Coleman, J. S., Campbell, E., Hobson, C., McPartland, J., Mood, A., & York, T. (1966). *Equality of educational opportunity.* Washington, DC: U.S. Government Printing Office.

Conti, S. D., Ellsasser, C. W., & Griffin, G. A. (2000). *School restructuring: A literature review.* New York: National Center for Restructuring Education, Schools, and Teaching.

Corcoran, T., Fuhrman, S. H., & Belcher, C. L. (2001). The district role in instructional improvement. *Phi Delta Kappan, 83*(1), 78–84.

Corcoran, T., & Wilson, B. (1989). *Successful secondary schools: Visions of excellence in American public schools.* London: Falmer Press.

Cotton, K. (2001). *School size, school climate, and student performance: Close-Up No. 20.* Portland, OR: Northwest Regional Educational Laboratory.

Covington, M. V. (1992). *Making the grade: A self-worth perspective on motivation and school reform.* New York: Cambridge University Press.

Daniel, L. G., & King, D. A. (1998). Knowledge and use of testing and measurement literacy of elementary and secondary teachers. *The Journal of Educational Research, 91*(6), 331–344.

Danielson, C. (1996). *Enhancing professional practice: A framework for teaching.* Alexandria VA: Association for Supervision and Curriculum Development.

Danielson, C., & McGreal, T. (2000). *Teacher evaluation to enhance professional practice.* Alexandria VA: Association for Supervision and Curriculum Development.

Darling-Hammond, L. (1997). *The right to learn: A blueprint for creating schools that work.* San Francisco, CA: Jossey-Bass Publishers.

Darling-Hammond, L., Ancess, J., & Falk, B. (1995). *Authentic assessment in action: Studies of schools and students at work.* New York: National Center for Restructuring Education, Schools, and Teaching.

DeBacker, T. K., & Nelson, R. M. (2000). Motivation to learn science: Differences related to gender, class type, and ability. *The Journal of Educational Research, 93*(4), 245–54.

Deci, E., & Ryan, R. M. (1994). Promoting self-determined education. *Scandinavian Journal of Educational Research, 38*(1), 3–14.

Dweck, C. S. (1986). Motivational processes affecting learning. *American Psychologist, 5,* 1179–1187.

Dweck, C. S., Goetz, T. E., & Strauss, N. L. (1980). Sex differences and learned helplessness: An experimental and naturalistic study of failure generalization and its mediators. *Journal of Personality and Social Psychology, 38,* 441–452.

Dweck, C. S., & Repucci, N. (1973). Learned helplessness and reinforcement responsibility in children. *Journal of Personality and Social Psychology, 25,* 109–116.

Education Trust Data Bulletin. (March 6, 2001). *The other gap: Poor students receive fewer dollars.* Washington, DC: Author.

Edmonds, R. (1979). Effective schools for the urban poor. *Educational Leadership, 37*(1), 15–27.

Edmonds, R. (1984). School effects and teacher effects. *Social Policy, 15,* 37–39.

Eichenstein, R. (1994). *Project Achieve, part 1: Qualitative findings, 1993–94.* Brooklyn, NY: Office of Educational Research, New York City Board of Education. (ERIC Document Reproduction Service No. ED 379 388)

Elder, L., & Paul, R. (2001). Critical thinking: Thinking with concepts. *Journal of Developmental Education, 24*(3), 42–43.

Elmore, R. F. (2000, Winter). *Building a new structure for school leadership.* Washington, DC: Albert Shanker Institute, Center for Policy Research in Education.

Elmore, R., & Burney, D. (1997). *Investing in teacher learning: Staff development and Instructional Improvement in Community School District 2, New York City.* New York: National Commission on Teaching and America's Future and the Consortium for Policy Research in Education.

Emmer, E. (1988). Praise and the instructional process. *Journal of Classroom Interaction, 23,* 32–39.

Epstein, J., & Connors, L. (1994). *Trust fund: School, family, and community partnerships in middle levels. Report No. 24.* Baltimore: Johns Hopkins University Center on Families, Communities, Schools, and Children's Learning.

Farber, S., & Finn, J. (2000, April). *The effect of small classes on student engagement.* Paper presented at the annual AREA meeting in New Orleans, LA.

Fasko, D., & Grubb, D. J. (1995). *The use of learner-centered principles test battery in preservice educational programs and in the school setting: Implications for teacher roles and professional development experiences.* (ERIC Document Reproduction Service No. ED 339 045)

Finn, J. (1998, May). Parental engagement that makes a difference. *Educational Leadership, 55*(8), 20–24.

Finn, J., & Achilles, C. (1990). Answers and questions about class size: A statewide experiment. *American Educational Research Journal, 27,* 557–577.

Fullan, M. (2000). The three stories of educational reform. *Phi Delta Kappan, 81*(8), 581–584.

Galletti, S. (1998, May). *Increasing the capacity and will to accelerate middle level reform.* Presented at the U.S. Department of Education's Early Adolescence Conference, Washington, DC.

Gamoran, A., Porter, A. C., Smithson, J., & White., P. A. (1997). Upgrading high school mathematics instruction: Improving learning opportunities for low-achieving, low-income youth. *Education Evaluation and Policy Analysis, 19*(4), 325–338.

Goldhaber, D. D., & Brewer, D. J. (1996). Evaluating the effect of teacher degree level on educational performance. *Developments in School Finance,* 199.

Good, T., & Weinstein, R. (1986). Schools make a difference: Evidence, criticisms, and new directions. *American Psychologist, 41*(10), 1090–1097.

Goodlad, J. I. (1984). *A place called school.* New York: McGraw-Hill.

Gould, E., Reeves, A., Graziano, M., & Gross, C. (1999). Neurogenesis in the neocortex of adult primates. *Science, 286,* 548–552.

Gregory, T. B., & Smith, G. R. (1987). *High schools as communities: The small school reconsidered.* Bloomington, IN: Phi Delta Kappa Foundation. (ERIC Document Reproduction Service No. ED 278 518)

Gunter, M. A., Estes, T., & Schwab, J. (1990). *Instruction: A models approach.* Boston: Allyn & Bacon.

Gurina, M., & Henley, P. (2001). *Boys and girls learn differently: A guide for teachers and parents.* San Francisco, CA: Jossey-Bass.

Hayton, M. (1998). Personal views of learning. *Mathematics Teaching, 162,* 17.

Holloway, J. H. (2001). Grouping students for increased achievement. *Educational Leadership, 59*(3), 84–85.

Horn, L., & Chen, X. (1998). *Toward resiliency: At-risk students who make it to college.* Washington, DC: Office of Educational Research and Improvement.

Howley, C. (1996). *Sizing up schooling: A West Virginia analysis and critique.* Unpublished doctoral dissertation, West Virginia University, Morgantown.

Hunter, M. (1982). *Teaching mastery.* El Segundo, CA: TIP Publications.

Johnson, D., Maruyama, G., Johnson, R., Nelson, D., & Skon, L. (1981). Effects of cooperative, competitive, and individualistic goal structures on achievement: A meta-analysis. *Psychological Bulletin, 89*(1), 47–62.

Johnson, D. W., & Johnson, R. T. (1999). *Learning together and alone: Cooperative, competitive, and individualistic learning.* Boston: Allyn & Bacon.

Johnson-Grooms, R. (1999). Recent research in pedagogy: Intrinsic versus extrinsic motivation. *The American Music Teacher, 49*(2), 58–59.

Kamins, M. L., & Dweck, C. S. (1999). Person versus process praise and criticism: Implications for contingent self-worth and coping. *Development Psychology, 35,* 835–847

Keedy, J., & Achilles, C. (1996, April). The need for school-constructed theories in practice in U.S. school restructuring. *Journal of Educational Administration, 35*(2), 102–122.

Keith, T., & Keith, P. (1993). *Integrating services for children and families: Understanding the past to shape the future.* New Haven, CT: Yale University Press.

Keller, J. (1983). Motivational design of instruction. In C. Reigheluth (Ed.), *Instructional-design theories and models: An overview of their current status.* Hillsdale, NJ: Erlbaum.

Kemperman, G., & Gage, F. (1999) New nerve cells for the adult brain. *Scientific American, 5,* 48.

Kershaw, C. A., & Blank, M. A. (1993, April). *Student and educator perceptions of the impact of an alternative school structure.* Paper presented at the Annual Meeting of the American Educational Research Association, Atlanta, GA. (ERIC Document Reproduction Service No. ED 360 729)

King, S. P. (1999). Leadership in the 21st century: Using feedback to maintain focus and direction. In D. D. Marsh (Ed.), *1999 ASCD Yearbook: Preparing our schools for the 21st century.* Alexandria, VA: Association for Supervision and Curriculum Development.

Kohn, A. (1993). Why incentive plans cannot work. *Harvard Business Review, 71*(5), 54–63.

Kruse, S. D. (1996, October). *Collaboration efforts among teachers: Implications for school administrators.* Paper presented at the Annual Meeting of the University Council for Educational Administrators, Louisville, KY.

Kulik, J. A. (1993, Spring). *An analysis of the research on ability grouping: Historical and contemporary perspectives.* Storrs, CT: The National Research Center on the Gifted and Talented.

Leikin, R., & Zaslavsky, O. (1997). Facilitating student interactions in mathematics in a cooperative learning setting. *Journal for Research in Mathematics Education, 28*(3), 331–354.

Lloyd, L. (1999). Multiage classes and high-ability students. *Review of Educational Research, 69*(2), 187–212.

Lou, Y., Abrami, P., & Spence, J. (2000). Effects of within-class grouping on student achievement: An exploratory model. *The Journal of Educational Research, 94*(2), 101–112.

Lou, Y., Abrami, P., Spence, J., Paulsen, C., Chambers, B., & d'Apollonio, S. (1996). Within class grouping: A meta-analysis. *Review of Educational Research, 66*(4), 423–458.

MacIver, D. J., & Prioleau, A. D. (1999). *Looping: Helping middle school teachers to be caring, daring and effective.* Paper presented at the Annual Meeting of American Educational Research Association, Montreal, Quebec.

MacIver, D. J., & Plank, S. B. (1997). Improving urban schools: Developing the talents of students placed at risk. In J. L. Irvin (Ed.), *What current research says to the middle level practitioner* (pp. 243–256). Columbus, OH: National Middle School Association.

Marsh, M. S. (1999). Life inside a school: Implications for reform in the 21st century. In D. D. Marsh (Ed.), *1999 ASCD Yearbook: Preparing our schools for the 21st century* (pp. 185–202).

Marshak, D. (1997). *Action research on block scheduling.* New York: Eye on Education.

Marshall, H. H., & Weinstein, R. S. (1984). Classroom factors affecting students: Self-evaluation: An interaction model. *Review of Educational Research, 54*(3), 301–25.

Marzano, R. J., Pickering, D. J., & Pollock, J. E. (2001). *Classroom instruction that works: Research-based strategies for increasing student achievement.* Alexandria, VA: Association for Supervision and Curriculum Development.

Mason, D., & Doepner, R. (1998). Principals' views of combination classes. *The Journal of Educational Research, 91*(3), 160–172.

McCarthy, S. J. (2000). Home-school connections: A review of the literature. *The Journal of Educational Research, 93*(3), 145–154.

McDonald, J. (1996). *Redesigning schools: Lessons for the 21st century.* San Francisco, CA: Jossey-Bass Publishers.

McLaughlin, H. J., & Doda, N. M. (1997). Teaching with time on your side: Developing long-term relationships in schools. In J. L. Irvin (Ed.), *What current research says to the middle level practitioner* (pp. 57–72). Columbus, OH: National Middle School Association.

McPartland, J., Balfanz, R., Jordan, W., & Legters, N. (1998). Improving climate and achievement in a troubled urban high school through the Talent Development Model. *Journal of Education for Students Placed At-Risk, 3*(4), 337–361.

McVey, M. D. (2001). Teacher praise: Maximizing the motivational impact. *Journal of Early Education and Family Review, 6*(4), 29–34.

Meece, J., & McColskey, W. (1997). *Improving student motivation: A guide for teachers and school improvement teams.* Tallahassee, FL: Southeastern Regional Vision for Education.

Meier, D. (1995). *The power of their ideas: Lessons for America from a small school in Harlem.* Boston: Beacon Press.

Mizell, M. H. (1994). *Focusing the middle school: The principal's role.* Presented at the Middle School Institute, Louisville, KY.

Mortimore, P. (1991). School effectiveness research: Which way at the crossroads? *International School Effectiveness and School Improvement, 2*(3), 213–229.

Mortimore, P. (1994). School effectiveness and the management of effective learning and teaching. *International School Effectiveness and School Improvement, 4*(4), 290–310.

Mosteller, F. (1995). The Tennessee study of class size in the early school grades. *Future of Children, 5*(2), 113–127.

Nanus, B. (1992). *Visionary leadership: Creating compelling sense of direction for your organization.* San Francisco, CA: Jossey-Bass Publishers.

National Commission on Excellence in Education. (1983). *A nation at risk: The imperative for educational reform.* Washington, DC: U.S. Government Printing Office.

National Commission on Teaching and America's Future. (1996). *What matters most: Teaching for America's future.* NY: Author.

Newmann, F. M., Rutter, R. A., & Smith, M. (1989). Organizational factors that affect school sense of efficacy, community, and expectations. *Sociology of Education, 62*(4), 221–238.

Newmann, F. M., & Wehlage, G. G. (1995). *Successful school restructuring: A report to the public.* Madision, WI: Center on Organization and Restructuring Schools.

Nichols, J. D., & Hall, N. (1995). *The effects of cooperative learning on student achievement and motivation in a high school geometry class.* Paper presented at the annual meeting of the American Educational Research Association, San Francisco. (ERIC Document Reproduction Service No. ED 387 341)

Nuthall, G. (1999). Learning how to learn: The evolution of students' minds through the social processes and culture of the classroom. *International Journal of Educational Research, 31*(3), 141–256.

Nyberg, K., McMillin, J., O'Neill-Rood, N., & Florence, F. (1997). Ethnic difference in academic retracking: A four-year longitudinal study. *The Journal of Educational Research, 91*(1), 33–41.

Oakes, J. (1985). *Keeping track: How schools structure inequality.* New Haven, CT: Yale University Press.

Ornstein, R. (1997). *The right mind.* Orlando, FL: Harcourt Brace.

Pfiffner, L. J., Rosen, L. A., & O'Leary, S. G. (1985). The efficacy of an all-positive approach to classroom management. *Journal of Applied Behavior Analysis, 18,* 257–261.

Porter, A. C., & Brophy, J. E. (1988). *The social world of the primary school.* London: Paul Elek.

Pressley, M., Yokoi, L., Rankin, J., Wharton-McDonald, R., & Mistretta, J. (1997). A survey of the instructional practices of grade-five teachers nominated as effective in promoting literacy. *Scientific Studies of Reading, 1*(2), 145–160.

Queen, J. A. (2000). Block scheduling revisited. *Phi Delta Kappan, 82*(3), 209–212.

Queen, J. A., Algozzine, R. F., & Eaddy, M. A. (1997). The road we traveled: Scheduling in the four-by-four block. *NASSP Bulletin, 81,* 88–99.

Queen, J. A., & Isenhour, K. G. (1998). *The four-by-four block schedule.* Princeton, NJ: Eye on Education.

Raywind, M. A. (1998). Small schools: A reform that works. *Educational Leadership, 55*(4), 34–38.

Reilly, D. (1995). *How to have successful schools.* Lanham, MD: University Press of America.

Riehl, C. (2000). The principal's role in creating inclusive schools for diverse students: A review of normative, empirical, and critical literature of the practice of educational administration. *Review of Educational Research, 70*(1), 55–81.

Rosenholtz, S. J. (1985). Effective schools: Interpreting the evidence. *American Journal of Education, 93,* 352–388.

Rosenthal, R. (1987). Pygmalion effects: Existence, magnitude, and social importance. *Educational Researcher, 16*(9), 37–41.

Rosenthal, R., & Jacobson, L. (1968). *Pygmalion in the classroom: Teacher expectations and pupils' intellectual development.* New York: Holt, Rinehart & Wilson.

Rutter, M., Maughan, B., Mortimore, P., & Ouston, J. (1979). *Fifteen thousand hours.* London: Open Books.

Sanders, W. L., & Horn, S. P. (1994). The Tennessee value-added assessment system (TVAAS): Mixed-added assessment methodology in educational assessment. *Journal of Personnel Evaluation in Education, 8,* 299–311.

Scheerens, J. (1992). *Effective schooling: Research, theory and practice.* London: Cassell.

Schroth, G., & Dixon, J. (1996). The effects of block scheduling on student performance. *International Journal of Educational Reform, 5,* 472–476.

Schunk, D. H. (1998). Teaching elementary students to self-regulate practice of mathematical skills with modeling. In D. H. Schunk & B. J. Zimmerman (Eds.), *Self-regulated learning: From teaching to self-refective practice* (pp. 137–159). New York: Guilford.

Senese, J. (2000, Winter). Data can help teacher to stand tall. *Journal of Staff Development, 21*(1), 84.

Sergiovanni, T. J. (1996). *Leadership for the schoolhouse: How is it different?* San Francisco, CA: Jossey-Bass.

Shartrand, A. M., Weiss, H. B., Kreider, H. M., & Lopez, M. E. (1997). *New skills for new schools: Preparing teachers in family involvement.* Cambridge, MA: Harvard Family Research Project, Harvard Graduate School of Education.

Sheppard, S., & Kanevsky, L. (1999). Nurturing gifted students' metacognitive awareness: Effects of training in homogenous and heterogeneous classes. *Roeper Review, 21*(4), 266–273.

Sizer, T. R. (1992). *Horace's compromise: The dilemma of the American high school* (3rd ed.). New York: Houghton Mifflin Co.

Skrobarcek, S. A. (1997). Collaboration for instructional improvement: Analyzing the academic impact of a block-scheduling plan. *NASSP Bulletin, 81,* 104–111.

Slavin, R. E. (1987). Ability grouping and student achievement in elementary schools: A best-evidence synthesis. *Review of Educational Research, 57,* 293–336.

Stevenson, H. W. (1990). *Making the grade in mathematics.* Reston, VA: National Council of Teachers of Mathematics.

Stigler, J. W., & Hiebert, J. (1999). *The teaching gap: Best ideas from the world's teachers for improving education in the classroom.* Free Press: New York.

Stockard, J., & Mayberry, M. (1992). *Effective educational environments.* Newbury Park, CA: Corwin Press.

Stringer, B. R., & Hurt, T. H. (1981). *To praise or not to praise: Factors to consider before utilizing praise as a reinforcing device in the classroom.* (ERIC Document Reproduction Service No. ED 202 054)

Taylor, B. M., Pressley, M., & Pearson, D. (2000). *Effective teachers and schools: Trends across recent studies.* Ann Arbor, MI: Center for Improvement of Early Reading Achievement, University of Michigan. (ERIC Document Reproduction Service No. ED 450 353)

Urdan, T. C., Midgley, C., & Anderman, E. M. (1998). The role of classroom goal structure in students' use of self-handicapping strategies. *American Educational Research Journal, 35*(1), 101–122.

Useem, E. (1998). *Teachers' appraisals of talent development: Middle school training, materials, and student progress* (Report No. 25). Baltimore, MD: Center for Research on the Education of Students Placed at Risk.

Viadero, D. (2001, October 3). Changing times: Despite its popularity, block scheduling's effect on learning remains unproven. *Education Week,* pp. 38–40.

Visher, M., & Hudis, P. (1999). *Aiming high: Strategies to promote high standards in schools.* Washington, DC: Office of Vocational and Adult Education, U.S. Department of Education.

Walberg, H. J. (1992). On local control: Is bigger better? In *Source book on school and district size, cost, and quality.* Minneapolis, MN: Minnesota University. (ERIC Document Reproduction Service No. ED 361 164)

Webb, N. M., Nemer, K. M., & Chizhik, A. W. (1998). Equity issues in collaborative group assessment: group composition and performance. *American Educational Research Journal, 35*(4), 607–651.

WestEd. (2001). *Independent Evaluation of the Beginning Teacher Support and Assessment Program (BTSA)* [Monograph]. San Francisco: Author.

White, P. A., Gamoran, A., Smithson, J., & Porter, A. C. (1996). Upgrading the high school mathematics curriculum: Math course-taking patterns in seven high schools in California and New York. *Educational Evaluation and Policy Analysis, 18,* 285–307.

Wilburn, K. T., & Felps, B. C. (1983). *Do pupil grading methods effect middle school students' achievement? A comparison of criterion-referenced versus norm-referenced evaluation.* (ERIC Document Reproduction Service No. ED 229 451)

Wilson, B. L., & Corbett, H. D. (1999). *No excuses: The eighth grade year in six Philadelphia middle schools.* Philadelphia: The Philadelphia Education Fund.

Wohlestetter, P., Mohrman, S. A., & Robertson, P. J. (1997). Successful school-based management: A lesson for restruc-turing urban schools. In D. Ravitch & J. P. Vitentti (Eds.), *New schools for a new century: The redesign of urban education* (pp. 201–225). New Haven, CT: Yale University Press.

Wolfe, P. (2001). *Brain matters: Translating research into classroom practice.* Alexandria, VA: Association of Supervision and Curriculum Development.

Wright, S. P., Horn, S. P., & Sanders, W. L. (1997). Teacher and classroom context effects on student achievement: Implications for teacher evaluation. *Journal of Personnel Evaluation in Education, 11,* 57–67.

Wynne, E. A., & Walberg, H. J. (1994). Persisting groups an overlooked force for learning. *Phi Delta Kappan, 75*(7), 527–528.

York, T. (1997). *A comparative analysis of student achievement in block and traditionally scheduled high schools.* Doctoral dissertation, University of Houston.

Index

Page references for figures are followed by *f*, as in 126*f*.

About the Author

Charlotte Danielson is an education consultant in Princeton, New Jersey. She has taught at all levels, from kindergarten through college; worked as a consultant on curriculum planning, performance assessment, and professional development for numerous schools and districts in the United States and overseas; and designed materials and training programs for ASCD, ETS, and the National Board for Professional Teaching Standards. She is the author of *Enhancing Professional Practice* (1996) and the coauthor with Tom McGreal of *Teacher Evaluation to Enhance Professional Practice* (2000), and can be reached by e-mail at charlotte_danielson@hotmail.com.

Related ASCD Resources

Books

Developing a Quality Curriculum by Allan A. Glatthorn (#194170)

The Diagnostic Teacher: Constructing New Approaches to Professional Development by Mildred Z. Solomon (#300269)

Enhancing Professional Practice: A Framework for Teaching by Charlotte Danielson (#196074)

Interdisciplinary Curriculum: Design and Implementation by David Ackerman, Heidi Hayes Jacobs, & David Perkins (#61189156)

More Strategies for Educating Everybody's Children by Bob Cole (#100229)

Audiotapes

Changing Curriculum Means Changing Your Mind by Arthur Costa (#200201)

Connecting the Curriculum Using an Integrated, Interdisciplinary, Thematic Approach by T. Roger Taylor (#297093)

Curriculum: Creating, Planning, and Designing for Quality by Paul Eggen, Giselle Martin-Kniep, David Grant, Rachel Lotan, & Susan Schultz (#299220)

Using Performance Tasks and Rubrics to Support Differentiated Instruction by Carolyn Callahan, Tonya Moon, & Carol Ann Tomlinson (#297069)

Videotapes

Curriculum Mapping: Charting the Course for Content by Heidi Hayes Jacobs (#499049)

Effective Schools for Children at Risk by James Comer, Richard Andrews, Larry Lezotte, & Robert Slavin (#614222)

Learning About Learning by Ron Brandt, Lauren Resnick, David Perkins, & Gaea Leinhardt (#614241)

The Understanding by Design Video Series, Tapes 1–3 by Grant Wiggins and Jay McTighe (#400241)

Multimedia

Analytic Processes for School Leaders Action Tool by Cynthia T. Richetti & Benjamin B. Tregoe (#701016)

Creating the Capacity for Change Action Tool by Jody Westbrook & Valarie Spiser-Albert (#702118)

Guide for Instructional Leaders Action Tool by Roland Barth, Bobb Darnell, Laura Lipton, & Bruce Wellman (#702110)

Standards for Excellence in Education Multimedia Kit (#798339)